Development Leads · Amanda Hamon Kunz and Joe Pasini

Authors · Emily Brumfield, Violet Hargrave, Susann Hessen, Mikko Kallio, Lyz Liddell, Adrian Ng, Joe Pasini, Lacy Pellazar, Kyle T. Raes, David N. Ross, and Kendra Leigh Speedling

Cover Artist · Chris Seaman

Interior Artists · Kent Hamilton, Forrest Imel, Litos Lopez Rodriguez, and Alyssa McCarthy

Creative Director · James Jacobs
Creative Design Director · Sarah E. Robinson
Executive Editor · James L. Sutter
Managing Developer · Adam Daigle
Development Coordinator · Amanda Hamon Kunz
Senior Developer · Robert G. McCreary
Organized Play Lead Developer · John Compton
Developers · Crystal Frasier, Jason Keeley, Mark Moreland, Joe Pasini, Owen K.C. Stephens, and Linda Zayas-Palmer
Managing Editor · Judy Bauer
Senior Editor · Christopher Carey
Editors · Lyz Liddell, Adrian Ng, and Lacy Pellazar
Lead Designer · Jason Bulmahn
Senior Designer · Stephen Radney-MacFarland
Designers · Logan Bonner and Mark Seifter
Art Director · Sonja Morris
Senior Graphic Designers · Emily Crowell and Adam Vick
Organized Play Coordinator · Tonya Woldridge

Publisher · Erik Mona
Paizo CEO · Lisa Stevens
Chief Operations Officer · Jeffrey Alvarez
Chief Financial Officer · John Parrish
Director of Sales · Pierce Watters
Sales Associate · Cosmo Eisele
Marketing Director · Jenny Bendel
Outreach Coordinator · Dan Tharp
Director of Licensing · Michael Kenway
Accountant · Christopher Caldwell
Data Entry Clerk · B. Scott Keim
Chief Technical Officer · Vic Wertz
Director of Technology · Dean Ludwig
Senior Software Developer · Gary Teter
Community & Digital Content Director · Chris Lambertz
Webstore Coordinator · Rick Kunz

Customer Service Team · Sharaya Copas, Katina Davis, Sara Marie, and Diego Valdez

Warehouse Team · Laura Wilkes Carey, Will Chase, Mika Hawkins, Heather Payne, Jeff Strand, and Kevin Underwood

Website Team · Lissa Guillet, Erik Keith, and Eric Miller

ON THE COVER

Seltyiel and the Red Raven ruin a wicked noble's evening with an ambush in this gorgeous cover art by Chris Seaman.

TABLE OF CONTENTS

REFERENCE

This Pathfinder Player Companion refers to several other Pathfinder Roleplaying Game products and uses the following abbreviations. These books are not required to make use of this Player Companion. Readers interested in references to Pathfinder RPG hardcovers can find the complete rules from these books available for free online at **paizo.com/prd**.

Advanced Class Guide	ACG	Ultimate Combat	UC
Advanced Player's Guide	APG	Ultimate Equipment	UE
Pathfinder Unchained	PU	Ultimate Magic	UM

Paizo Inc.
7120 185th Ave NE, Ste 120
Redmond, WA 98052-0577

paizo.com

Introduction

A kindhearted assassin, a paladin with a mean streak she's trying to beat, a summoner who serves justice but really only wants to get paid—these are not the shining knights that the word "hero" brings to mind. No matter their backstories, antiheroes are a bit jaded, a little skewed, or at least somewhat offbeat. They count among their number characters such as a psychic warrior from faraway Vudra who comes to Avistan to seek riches while doing occasional good deeds along the way, a Chelish diabolist desperately looking for a way to unsell his soul, and an unlikely Desnan from a riverside village staunchly devoted to Ghlaunder, demigod of parasites and disease, who just wants to sate her wanderlust but sometimes rescues other innocents from the evil clutches of her hometown's priests.

In this volume, you will find rules and guidelines to bring these and many other antiheroes to your campaign.

WHAT MAKES AN ANTIHERO?

A true hero is someone who does the right thing for the right reason. She has selfless motivations and fights for selfless causes, though she can still look out for her own interests. If she gets rich deposing a ruthless tyrant, that's fine. But saving the lich ruler's people is still her main goal; wealth is just a bonus.

But what if that equation changes slightly? What if she just wants to get paid? Or what if she instead serves a powerful undead creature because the ruler protects her people from a mighty nearby threat? Or what if the protagonist of the story is the lich herself, not the would-be liberator? Then the story takes on a new aspect, and an antihero takes the stage.

In the Pathfinder Roleplaying Game, an antihero is an adventurer who works with the other members of her party on uneasy terms—but still works with them. The antihero might have her own motivations, side schemes, or backstabbing contingencies, but as long as her goals line up with those of the other party members, she's a valuable member of the team.

Vengeance is perhaps the most iconic antihero motivation. The lich ruler who wants revenge on a marilith who slaughtered her serfs has good reason to work with a powerful group of wandering heroes, maintaining an uneasy truce and making sure to give them no reason to turn on her.

The acquisition of wealth and power is another classic driving motivation of those who perform heroic deeds for less-than-heroic reasons. It's a good bet that a Gorumite mercenary who cares for nothing but the money will still honor whatever code of conduct his contract stipulates to uphold his employers' reputation—so long as the gold keeps flowing.

Even truly evil creatures can feel loyalty. An ogre mage who owes her life to a party member can make a stalwart

2

compatriot, even if she thinks the things her savior asks of her are silly and pointless. Conversely, a cavalier's brother who joined the Red Mantis assassins might take it upon himself to take care of the dirty business his little brother doesn't realize he needs to have done, thus protecting the cavalier's innocence.

And then there are those who desperately desire to be good but fall miserably short of their goals. An orc warrior escaped from her murderous hold might have the strongest will in the world, but she might still find that morality is a difficult concept to master. A priest of the magic-loving god Nethys might idolize spellcasting to the point of allowing harm to befall those he is supposed to protect in favor of creating the mightiest magical explosions.

ANTIHEROES ON GOLARION

While antiheroes share some common characteristics, their backgrounds are vast and varied. For every type of hero, there is an antihero waiting in the shadows, ready to start adventuring.

In Varisia, where stories resonate deeply, legends from the present day all the way back to the time of ancient Thassilon and earlier fall from the lips of storytellers like fondly recalled memories. Here, wide-eyed youngsters from the nomadic Shoanti quahs or the rough-and-tumble streets of the nation's teeming towns and cities might just decide that they want a legend of their own and set off to find a worthy adventure.

Geb is the land of the dead, but even there, stories of heroic adventurers and their daring deeds are popular among dreamers and idealists. An enthusiastic young noble is an archetypal adventurer background, and that does not change just because the youngster is a dhampir.

Baba Yaga's granddaughters patrol Irrisen, keeping the peasantry's hearts coated in ice-cold fear. But even the winter witches have souls, and not all are so tied to the Queen of Witches. Some few of these witches have developed a regard for their people, both because it pleases them and because they have something resembling fondness for their subjects.

The Aspis Consortium breeds treachery and exploitation, but not everything it does is vicious. Sometimes, sheer pragmatism means that an act that supports the Consortium also does some good in the world. When this happens, a charismatic and likable Aspis agent might approach an adventuring party with a deal. Some such associations turn into long-term affairs—though trusting an Aspis agent is a tall order indeed!—and a few agents have even ended up cutting ties with their former colleagues in favor of their new friends.

As a rule, Hellknight orders are not full of kindly individuals, but those knights who value virtue above evil are hardly uncommon. Some are even good-hearted souls, seeing in their group a dedication to protecting others from the predators of society.

In deep Hagegraf in Nar-Voth, toil is sacred and the general consensus is that wanderlust is flighty and irresponsible. It is no wonder, then, that some independent-minded duergar leave their society behind, choosing adventure over the evil god Droskar. While not common, some duergar warriors find their way into the adventuring profession, and even though they have forsaken the Dark Smith, these exiles often find surface society lazy, soft, and disapproving.

RULES INDEX

The following new rules options in this Pathfinder Player Companion are located on the indicated pages.

Several archetypes presented in this book are usable by ex-members of specific classes; for a full rules explanation, see page 12.

Antiheroic Backgrounds

It can be easy for adventurers who have led charmed lives to take on the mantle of hero and face adversity with courage and virtue. However, those who achieve heroic ends through less-than-valiant means are often defined by their darker pasts. The following backgrounds, traits, and drawbacks use the character background generator rules found starting on page 16 of *Pathfinder RPG Ultimate Campaign*.

ANTIHEROIC ORIGINS

You can choose a background from one of the tables below, or you can select a table and roll randomly to determine your background. If you choose an antiheroic origin, do so during Step 2 of the process described on page 16 of

Ultimate Campaign, before or in place of rolling to determine an influential associate.

Each background grants access to some combination of traits or drawbacks; gaining or taking a drawback typically entitles a character to a free third trait, although the appropriate number of traits and drawbacks for a character is up to your GM. If your chosen antiheroic origin gives you a drawback, at your GM's discretion, skip choosing a second drawback during Step 3 of background generation.

CRIMINAL BACKGROUNDS

The following backgrounds represent individuals who were living ordinary lives until they crossed the law, intentionally or not. Roll on the table below to determine which miscarriage of justice made you forever distrustful of society's eagerness to uphold the letter of the law.

d%	Result
1–15	**Biased Liberator:** You broke a friend or loved one out of jail, believing her to be innocent of the crime for which she were imprisoned. You bought her freedom, but it was at the price of your own; you will be locked up if you ever return home. You gain access to the Fugitive combat trait (see page 7).
16–30	**Body Double:** A bandit who bore an uncanny resemblance to you committed a terrible crime, and your lack of alibi combined with an unfair trial meant that you were wanted dead or alive in the place you once called home. You gain access to the Fugitive combat trait (see page 7).
31–45	**Ignorant Tourist:** While traveling abroad, you committed what would be a minor offense in your homeland, but you were severely punished for it under strict local laws. You gain access to the Callous social trait (see page 7).
46–65	**Oppressed Herbalist:** You are an expert at cultivating a rare plant that has a variety of medicinal qualities, but local superstitions led to it being outlawed, and you were ostracized along with the plant. You gain access to the Stigmatized drawback (see page 6).
66–80	**Stood Your Ground:** A community member with a sterling public reputation secretly preyed upon you or a loved one, until one day you killed the wretch in self defense. However, your reasoning fell on willfully ignorant ears, and you were treated as a cold-blooded murderer. You gain access to the Bitter drawback (see page 6).
81–100	**Tried as an Adult:** As a child, you accepted a dare to steal an object of local import. You were caught in the act, and your elders decided to make an example of you, tarnishing your reputation through to adulthood. You gain access to the Stigmatized drawback (see page 6).

ORGANIZATION BACKGROUNDS

Whether maligned by malicious groups or unintentionally aggrieved by well-meaning ones, many antiheroes have been shaped by the world's powerful organizations. Roll on the table below to determine the organization that helped forge your less traditionally heroic personality.

d%	Result
1–15	**Collateral Damage:** You had a successful business in a small crossroads town until a group of swaggering Pathfinders delved into a local underground ruin and removed a powerful artifact, unaware that it had been placed there to contain a terrible evil. They eventually defeated the unleashed threat, but not before the town—and your livelihood—were utterly destroyed. You gain access to the Cynical social trait (see page 7).
16–30	**Hellknight Hounded:** You and your people were driven from your homeland after Hellknights of the Order of the Nail deemed you uncivilized. The experience instilled in you a hatred of all the trappings of civilization—and especially of people who look down on those they consider less cultured. You gain access to the Contemptuous social trait (see page 7).
31–45	**High Price of Freedom:** You lived a hard but contented life as the serf of a benevolent dictator until a contingent of the Eagle Knights' Golden Legion traveled through your native lands, espousing democracy and freedom. Your fellow serfs took the message to heart and seized power for themselves, but the resultant regime soon fell to corruption and infighting, leaving you with no home and a deep distrust of radical change. You gain access to the Cynical social trait (see page 7).
46–65	**Maiden Scarred:** As a child, you fell to the care of a former member of the Erinyes Company of the Gray Maidens. She forced upon you the psychological conditioning she had endured in her service to Queen Ileosa and even went so far as to scar your face before you were able to escape. You gain access to the Scarred drawback (see page 6).
66–80	**Orphan of the Mantis:** Your prominent parents became entangled in local politics while trying to forge a better life for your family. This earned them a powerful enemy—one who contracted a Red Mantis assassin to murder them. You gain access to the Vengeful social trait (see page 7).
81–100	**Dishonored Thief:** As the eldest of several children in an impoverished Chelish family, you resorted to desperate measures to ensure your siblings' survival, eventually stealing food and clothing for them. An agent of the Council of Thieves offered to pay you well for a simple heist, and you agreed—only to be caught in a sting arranged by the tightly controlled criminal organization, which had not taken kindly to your unauthorized thefts. You gain access to the Dirty Trickster combat trait (see page 7).

RELIGIOUS BACKGROUNDS

While religions often provide their worshipers something greater than themselves to focus on, the tenets of virtually any faith can provide a bitter, searching soul with all the justification needed to pursue a course that suits less-than-honorable predilections. Roll on the table below to determine which god spoke to your soul's less charitable aspects.

d%	Result
1–15	**Contracted Servant:** As an arrogant youth, you signed a contract with an agent of Asmodeus for a short-term benefit, unaware of the soul-damning acts you had agreed to perform. You commit these heinous acts in secret while looking desperately for a way out of the deal. You gain access to the Solitary combat trait (see page 7) and Haunted drawback (see page 6).
16–30	**Drunken Antihero:** When a personal tragedy struck, you intensified your formerly moderated worship of Cayden Cailean and began to drink to excess, turning your once-celebratory drinking into an often self-destructive act. You gain access to the Obnoxious social trait (see page 7).
31–45	**Unbound Appetite:** Growing up alone in the streets, you learned that life could be brutally short, and you determined never to pass up an opportunity to satisfy an appetite, be it emotional or gastronomic. A worshiper of Urgathoa nurtured these tendencies until you too began to worship the goddess of gluttony. You gain access to the Insatiable drawback (see page 6).
46–65	**Living Vengeance:** You were left for dead by your closest companions, and in seeking vengeance you were drawn to worship Calistria. You mostly ignore her hedonistic aspects and instead focus on exacting your revenge, not only against your betrayers but also against those who even remotely resemble them, whether in appearance or behavior. You gain access to the Vengeful social trait (see page 7).
66–80	**Magically Inclined:** You were drawn to Nethys early in life thanks to your thirst for magical power and utter disregard for its consequences. Those close to you quickly realized that you were just as likely to harm them as help them with your abilities, which made it difficult for you to form lasting relationships. You gain access to the Solitary combat trait (see page 7).
81–100	**Traditionalist:** Your worship of Erastil has led you to venture into the world in order to provide for your community, but it has also implanted a firm mistrust of society outside your home. You don't suffer fools gladly, and you consider most who are not from your part of the world to be fools. You gain access to the Contemptuous social trait (see page 7).

TRAGIC BACKGROUNDS

Whereas some heroes have greatness thrust upon them, many antiheroes are scarred by some terrible event that they carry with them like a heavy stone. Roll on the table

below to determine which trauma from the past darkens your every step.

d%	Result
1–15	**Child of Freedom:** Your parents were influential leaders in a group of underground freedom fighters until their role was discovered, and you were forced to watch as they were brutally and publicly executed for their crimes. You gain access to the Helpless drawback (see below).
16–30	**Infestation:** You went to stay with reclusive relatives as a child, but when you arrived, you found them dead and engulfed by swarming vermin—and you barely escaped sharing their fate. You gain access to the Entomophobe drawback (see below).
31–45	**Heirless Parent:** The first decades of your life were full of joy and family, but you saw each of your many children die from various misfortunes and tragedies, and you are now the sole surviving member of your once-large family. You gain access to the Callous social trait (see page 7).
46–65	**Magic Scarred:** A powerful and avaricious magic-user unwittingly caused an explosion of transmuting magic that enveloped your entire town, turning most of its residents into abominable horrors that you and the other mutated survivors had to put down. You gain access to the Scarred drawback (see below).
66–80	**Sole Survivor:** You lived peacefully in a small village until an encroaching monstrous threat began to destroy nearby communities. You were sent to seek help, but every supposed hero you could find rebuffed you. By the time you returned, everyone you loved had been obliterated by a ravenous horde. You gain access to the Cynical social trait (see page 7) and the Haunted drawback (see below).
81–100	**Unlucky Sailor:** You eagerly joined a ship's crew in your youth, but it sank on its first voyage, stranding you for days in the unforgiving sea. You watched as many of your fellow sailors died of hypothermia or were dragged beneath the waves by unseen beasts, until finally a passing ship rescued you. You gain access to the Callous social trait (see page 7) and the Helpless drawback (see below).

ANTIHEROIC DRAWBACKS

Most antiheroes are driven as much by the burdens they carry as they are by their passions. Full rules for drawbacks can be found on page 64 of *Pathfinder RPG Ultimate Campaign*. When you use the background generator process described on page 16 of that book, use these drawbacks in place of the presented drawbacks. Choose one, or roll 1d10 to determine your antihero's drawback.

Bitter: You have been hurt repeatedly by those you trusted, and it has become difficult for you to accept help. When you receive healing from an ally's class feature, spell, or spell-like ability, reduce the amount of that healing by 1 hit point.

Cowardly: You might face dangerous situations with bravado, but you are constantly afraid. Your base speed when frightened and fleeing increases by 5 feet, and the penalties you take from having the cowering, frightened, panicked, or shaken conditions increase by 1. If you would normally be immune to fear, you do not take these penalties but instead lose your immunity to fear (regardless of its source).

Entomophobe: A harrowing experience with insects when you were young instilled in you a deep-seated fear of vermin of all description, especially when they swarm together. You take a –2 penalty on attacks against vermin, and you take a –2 penalty on saving throws against the nauseated condition of a swarm's distraction ability.

Haunted: Something from your past—or a dark secret you presently hold—makes it difficult for you to ever be at peace, and your chronic worry that you might fall to evil influence has become a self-fulfilling prophecy. You take a –2 penalty on saves against spells with the evil descriptor.

Helpless: You once stood helpless as great harm befell a loved one, and that paralysis sometimes returns when an ally is in a dire position. The first time per combat encounter that an ally within 30 feet falls unconscious or dies as the result of an attack, you are dazed until the end of your next turn.

Impatient: You love leaping into battle at the earliest opportunity, and it frustrates you to wait for others to act. You can't delay or ready actions, and if you are the last of your allies to act in a round of combat, you take a –1 penalty on ability checks, attack rolls, saving throws, and skill checks.

Insatiable: You have become so accustomed to binging on the finer things in life that you find going without such excess particularly strenuous. Goods and services cost you 10% more (and can't be paid for by allies), and you need twice as much food and liquid as normal for the purposes of preventing starvation and thirst (*Pathfinder RPG Core Rulebook* 444).

Scarred: An injury left you horribly, visibly scarred, making it more difficult for you to hide your true face, and also making most people distrustful of you merely due to your appearance. You take a –5 penalty on Disguise checks and a –2 penalty on Bluff checks.

Self-Doubting: Your ever-present fear of failure causes a downward spiral. The first time each day that you fail a Will saving throw or skill check, you take a –2 penalty on the next Will saving throw or skill check of that kind.

Stigmatized: You were kept at the periphery of society for a long period of time, so that even when you are among strangers in a new place, you feel the weight of your missing socialization. You take a –3 penalty on Diplomacy checks to gather information or improve a creature's attitude.

ANTIHEROIC TRAITS

Antiheroes play by their own internal rules that allow them to accomplish things that those with stricter moral codes (or weaker stomachs) might not. Full rules for traits can be found beginning on page 326 of *Pathfinder RPG Advanced Player's Guide*. The list to which each trait belongs is indicated in parentheses.

Callous (Social): You have endured many hardships throughout your life, and this has hardened you to the suffering of others to the point that you are not easily swayed by a sad story. You gain a +4 trait bonus on Sense Motive checks that oppose the Bluff checks of creatures that attempt to deceive you by winning your sympathy.

Contemptuous (Social): Whether you are a commoner who has come to despise the haughty upper crust or a holier-than-thou noble who can't stand being around the unwashed masses, your contempt drives you to study carefully, making sure you always have the upper hand in social exchanges with them. You gain a +1 trait bonus on Knowledge (local) checks and Knowledge (nobility) checks, and one of these skills becomes a class skill for you.

Criminally Connected (Social): You have spent a lot of time dealing with the criminal underworld—so much that it might be hard for observers to see you as distinct from it. However, this familiarity gives you a leg up on heroes who refuse to muddy their reputation. While in settlements, you gain a +1 trait bonus on Knowledge (local) checks and on Diplomacy checks to gather information.

Cynical (Social): You have seen many heroes in your time, but you see only their capacity for failure and the ways they fall short of being truly good. This practice in looking past facades has proven a useful skill. You gain a +1 trait bonus on saving throws against illusions and charm effects.

Dirty Trickster (Combat): You learned early that there's no point in fighting fair when you're fighting for your life. Others may look down their noses at your tactics, but you know you wouldn't have survived this long without breaking a few conventions of fair play. You can take the Improved Dirty Trick^APG feat without meeting its prerequisites, and you gain a +1 trait bonus on combat maneuver checks to attempt a dirty trick^APG.

Fugitive (Combat): You crossed the law (or those in charge thought you did), and you are now a wanted criminal. As such, you have grown used to looking over your shoulder wherever you go. While in settlements, you gain a +3 trait bonus on Perception checks to determine awareness for the purpose of a surprise round.

Irreverent (Faith): You are suspicious of those who lead spiritual lives and are quick to seek out the smallest hypocrisy in even the most pious individuals. Of course, you are also keenly aware of the power the faithful can draw from their worship, and you are stubbornly resistant to it. You gain a +2 trait bonus on saving throws against divine spells that target only you.

Obnoxious (Social): You have long since forgotten to care what people think about you—though your interactions are always memorable, at the very least. Choose Perform (act), Perform (comedy), Perform (oratory), or Perform (sing); you gain a +1 trait bonus on checks with the chosen skill and gain it as a class skill.

Solitary (Combat): You are skilled at slipping away from crowds. Once per day, you can attempt a Bluff check to create a diversion to hide with a +2 trait bonus on the check, and if successful, you take only a –5 penalty on your Stealth check to get to an unobserved place while observers are distracted (instead of the normal –10 penalty).

Spirit of the Law (Combat): You have seen the rules of society endlessly twisted in their implementation, and as such, you are especially wary of those who exploit the law to impose their own will. You gain a +1 trait bonus on attacks against lawful-aligned humanoids and a +2 trait bonus on saving throws against effects with the lawful descriptor.

Vengeful (Social): You were brutally betrayed, and you have dedicated yourself to pursuing revenge. Choose a humanoid subtype that is not your own from the following list: dwarf, elf, gnome, halfling, or human. You gain a +2 trait bonus on Intimidate checks against creatures with that subtype.

Dastardly Adventurers

Among the common folk of the world, there exists a steadfast image of a noble hero—a brave adventurer with gleaming armor and a sharpened sword outstretched, her posture unwavering in the face of those who would oppose all that is good. A prayer to Iomedae, Lady of Valor, or perhaps Sarenrae, the Cleansing Light, falls from her lips as quickly as vows to protect the innocent, and doing the right thing is always compensation enough.

An antihero, however, is no such paragon.

Some antiheroes are good at heart, but circumstances have forced them to abandon higher ideals, if indeed they ever held ideals in the first place. Others are disillusioned with society altogether and see little value in fighting for an uncaring world—unless it's profitable. Still other antiheroes have noble intentions but morally questionable methods. For all antiheroes, the world is draped in shades of gray, and a call for heroes is one they surely don't immediately answer.

Because of the unusual lives they lead, many antiheroes command unique abilities that make them valuable allies despite shortcomings in their bravery, dedication, morality, or skills. Antiheroes may be reluctant to work alongside typical heroes, and the feeling is often mutual, but dire circumstances or temporarily aligned interests can convince them to put aside the different perspectives and mistrust that usually keep them apart. These unconventional adventurers might not be the most reliable, selfless, or valiant members of a group, but they are often the best at surviving to see another day—and helping their friends do so, as well.

Some adventurers would be doomed to fail without the help of an antihero, who has fewer moral compunctions than most to do what is necessary to get the job done. Some heroes may see the good in their shadier counterparts and believe they can redeem these lost souls, or at least channel their destructive energies toward a higher purpose. With time, heroes and antiheroes can earn each other's grudging admiration, and perhaps even accept that the world needs both kinds.

FLAWED FEATS

Antiheroes are conflicted individuals who often struggle internally with challenges such as indecision, recklessness, stubbornness, or vindictiveness. These personality flaws rarely go away, but some antiheroes learn to control them. The following new feats allow flawed characters to turn their weaknesses into strengths at opportune times. Some of the feats below provide a benefit after failing a saving throw; as normal, it is possible to voluntarily fail a saving throw in order to gain such a feat's benefit.

BLOODY MESS (COMBAT)
Your recklessness often puts you in harm's way, and you are terrifying to behold when covered in your own blood.

Prerequisite: Skill Focus (Intimidate).

Benefit: Whenever you take an amount of piercing, slashing, or bleed damage equal to or greater than double your character level, you can attempt an Intimidate check as an immediate action to demoralize the creature that dealt the damage as long as it is within 30 feet of you. If the damage resulted from a critical hit, you can cause the target creature to be sickened instead of shaken if you successfully demoralize it. You can use this feat only once per round to attempt an Intimidate check to demoralize an opponent.

DECEITFUL INCOMPETENCE (COMBAT)
You learn from your mistakes rapidly when others lower their guard around you.

Prerequisite: Combat Reflexes.

Benefit: When you make an attack of opportunity in a single round after you have already made an unsuccessful attack of opportunity that round, you gain a cumulative +2 insight bonus on your attack roll for each unsuccessful attack of opportunity. For example, if you have made one unsuccessful attack of opportunity and an enemy provokes another attack of opportunity from you during that same round, you gain a +2 insight bonus on that attack roll, and if you have made two unsuccessful attacks of opportunity in a round and an enemy provokes another attack of opportunity from you during that same round, you gain a +4 insight bonus on that attack roll, and so on.

OPPORTUNISTIC GRAPPLER (COMBAT)

When someone grabs you, you can easily reach that opponent's vulnerable spots.

Benefit: While you are grappled (but not when you are controlling the grapple), you can attempt a dirty trick^{APG} combat maneuver against the creature grappling you without provoking an attack of opportunity or taking a penalty on the combat maneuver check. If you have the Improved Dirty Trick^{APG} feat, you gain a +2 bonus on combat maneuver checks to attempt such a dirty trick, and the condition the dirty trick imposes lasts for 1 round longer than normal. This bonus stacks with the bonuses granted by Improved Dirty Trick and Greater Dirty Trick^{APG} feats.

SHELTERING STUBBORNNESS

Your stubborn mind is not easy to sway.

Prerequisite: Iron Will.

Benefit: When you fail a saving throw against a mind-affecting effect with a duration of 1 round or longer (such as *confusion*), you can choose to be dazzled for the first round of the duration instead of suffering the usual effect. On subsequent rounds, the effect functions normally. If an effect, immunity, or other ability prevents you from being dazzled, this feat has no effect.

VINDICTIVE FALL

When you fall, you drag others down with you.

Prerequisite: Lightning Reflexes.

Benefit: When a creature causes you to fall prone, such as with an effect or a spell (such as *grease*) or by succeeding at a combat maneuver to trip you, you can attempt a combat maneuver check as an immediate action to trip an enemy within your melee reach. The target of this combat maneuver need not be the creature that caused you to fall prone. If you do not have the Improved Trip feat or a similar ability, your trip combat maneuver provokes an attack of opportunity from the target as normal.

BLATHERSKITE (GUNSLINGER ARCHETYPE)

A blatherskite talks big and feels powerful when holding a loaded gun, but when the gun jams or the situation gets too intense, he's the first to run for cover. He has an extraordinary talent for retreating from harm's way and fooling his enemies into thinking he is weaker than he is.

Class Skills: A blatherskite gains Escape Artist and Stealth as class skills, but he doesn't gain Handle Animal and Intimidate as class skills.

This alters the gunslinger's class skills.

Deeds: A blatherskite swaps four deeds for the following.

Blatherskite's Stagger (Ex): At 1st level as an immediate action, when a ranged attack would normally miss a blatherskite, he can allow it to hit him and dramatically stagger a few steps backward, moving up to 10 feet directly away from the attacker. This movement provokes attacks of opportunity as normal. The attack deals the minimum amount of damage (as though the attacker had rolled a natural 1 on each damage die).

At 2nd level, if a ranged attack hits the blatherskite but the attack roll exceeds his AC by no more than his bonus from the nimble class feature, he can spend 1 grit point as an immediate action to take the minimum amount of damage and move up to 10 feet directly away from the attacker. This movement provokes attacks of opportunity as normal.

The gunslinger can perform this deed only while wearing medium or light armor and while carrying no more than a light load.

This deed replaces the gunslinger's dodge deed.

Blatherskite's Initiative (Ex): At 3rd level, the blatherskite gains benefits as long as he has at least 1 grit point. The blatherskite gains a +2 bonus on initiative checks. Furthermore, if he is trained in Stealth (and as long as he is not paralyzed, prone, or otherwise immobilized), he can take a 5-foot step and attempt a Stealth check to hide as part of the initiative check, provided there is an object or a larger creature to hide behind; if he spends 1 grit point, he can move up to half his speed instead of taking only a 5-foot step as part of the initiative check.

This deed replaces the gunslinger initiative deed.

Cheap Shot (Ex): At 3rd level, if the blatherskite has at least 1 grit point and makes a successful attack against an unarmed target with a firearm that is not making a scattering shot, he deals 1d6 additional points of damage. This is precision damage and is not multiplied on a critical hit.

This deed replaces the pistol-whip deed.

Blatherskite's Surprise (Ex): At 7th level, when the blatherskite succeeds at a saving throw against a spell or an effect that would cause him to be blinded, confused, dazed, fascinated, frightened, nauseated, paralyzed, or stunned, he can allow the effect to affect him normally. As long as he has at least 1 grit point, as an immediate action he can cause the creature from which the effect originated to lose its Dexterity bonus to AC for a number of rounds equal to half the duration of the effect (in rounds) or half the gunslinger's level, whichever is lower (minimum 1 round). If he instead spends 1 grit point, he does not need to allow the effect to affect him normally to use this deed.

This deed replaces the startling shot deed.

Faulty Teamwork

Antiheroes don't always go it alone; after all, companions provide added muscle and better protection, and they can often be persuaded to do the heavy lifting or employ their skills to help the antihero further her own goals. But many adventurers fear that an antihero will turn on them at a critical moment or that she is using them only for her own gain—such as a disguised Red Mantis assassin using the party as a means to reach a target that she would find difficult to corner alone.

However, antiheroes can nonetheless prove to be valuable allies. Their morally gray perspectives lead them to consider options that might not occur to other characters, and they are less likely to flinch at taking on unseemly tasks that more straight-laced members of the party might shy away from. A Sczarni agent might not think twice about using entrapment and blackmail to force an opponent to aid her allies, whereas more upright characters might balk at doing so themselves.

Whatever opinions other party members might have of the antihero, her efforts ultimately remain focused on her own goals. It isn't uncommon for a member of the Sleepless Agency to join up with an adventuring party traveling to the same town, nor is it uncommon for her to pitch in and help the group out along the way, but should their goals conflict upon the group's arrival, the antihero won't hesitate to turn her investigative skills upon them. Likewise, a Sczarni trader might fight fiercely to protect his companions (and their treasures) from bandits, but savvy travelers know to keep a hand on their coin purses around him, lest they suddenly lighten.

FLAWED TEAMWORK FEATS

While most teamwork feats rely on cooperation and mutual benefit, the antihero relies on feats that boost his abilities at the cost of his allies—but often with outcomes so advantageous that the ally is hard pressed to refuse aid.

Casting Conduit (Teamwork)

You can use an ally as a conduit to convey spells to an enemy she can touch.

Prerequisite: Spellcraft 1 rank.

Benefit: When casting a spell with a range of touch that deals hit point damage, you can target a willing, adjacent ally who also has this feat. The ally takes the minimum damage from the spell, and as an immediate action the ally can make a touch attack against an adjacent foe to deliver the spell. If this attack hits, the spell deals its normal damage to the opponent. If the ally has the grappled or pinned condition, the spell is automatically transferred to the grappling or grappled foe with no attack roll needed. This ability has no effect if the targeted ally is immune to the spell's effect (such as *shocking grasp* delivered to an ally immune to electricity).

Designated Antagonist (Teamwork)

When you antagonize your foes, you can redirect their enmity to your ally.

Prerequisite: Antagonize[UM].

Benefit: When you succeed at a skill check using Antagonize, you can cause the target creature to focus its efforts on a willing ally who also has this feat, as if the ally had been the one to use the ability.

Fall Guy (Teamwork)

Your ally plays the part of a bumbling fool, making you look good in comparison.

Prerequisite: Bluff 1 rank.

Benefit: An ally who also has this feat can spend a standard action bumbling around, uttering gaffes, or otherwise making herself appear to be socially inept. The ally takes a –2 penalty on future Charisma-based checks against characters who witnessed her behavior, but you gain a +2 competence bonus on such checks. The penalty and bonus both end after 24 hours.

Piercing Gambit (Teamwork)

You cast a spell destined to fail in order to help your ally overcome an enemy's spell resistance.

Prerequisites: Spell Penetration or Bluff 3 ranks; caster level 1st.

Benefit: You can expend one prepared spell or spell slot, as if you had cast the spell, to weaken an enemy's defenses. Your spell has no effect, but a designated ally who also has this feat gains a bonus on her caster level check to overcome spell resistance equal to half the level of the spell or spell slot you expended, lasting until the start of your next turn.

Sacrificial Aid (Teamwork)

You convince an ally to help you disable a trap, but the ally takes the damage if you fail.

Benefit: When you attempt to disable a trap, an ally who also has this feat can bolster your efforts. The ally rolls 1d20 and adds either her total bonus on Disable Device checks or her character level, whichever is higher; if the result of the ally's roll is 10 or greater, you gain a +4 bonus on your Disable Device check. If you trigger the trap, your ally is the target of the trap's effects. In the case of a trap with multiple targets, your ally takes the effects both for herself and for you (potentially taking damage twice or attempting saving throws twice).

Normal: You can use the aid another action only if you are able to attempt the skill check in question. The bonus provided is only +2.

Spell Bluff (Teamwork)

When your ally is in the area of effect of a harmful spell, your foes are caught off guard.

Benefit: When an ally who also has this feat fails her saving throw (including voluntarily failing the save) against a spell that would harm her with an area of effect that includes her, intelligent enemies within the spell's area take a –2 penalty on their saving throws to resist the spell's effects.

Take This (Teamwork)

You can quickly retrieve items from the body of a companion who is unable to act.

Benefit: If you are adjacent to an ally who also has this feat but is unable to act, you can retrieve a held or openly carried item from his body as a swift action that does not provoke attacks of opportunity.

Normal: Retrieving a stored item or picking up a fallen item is a move action that provokes attacks of opportunity.

Special: This is an exception to the rule that allies who are unable to act do not count for the purpose of teamwork feats.

COLLUDING SCOUNDREL (HUNTER ARCHETYPE)

The colluding scoundrel is a canny and conniving skirmisher, manipulating her enemies and leveraging her allies for her own benefit. A Free Captain ordering her crew to occupy foes and thus expose the enemy to her attacks might take this archetype, and colluding scoundrels have proven to be formidable members of the Wasp Queens, as their giant wasp companions draw out opponents to fall under the Wasp Queens' stinging blades. In any case, the colluding scoundrel rarely concerns herself overmuch with her allies' well-being.

Scapegoat (Ex): A colluding scoundrel is adept at redirecting a foe's hostility toward another creature, creating openings for her own attacks. A number of times per day equal to her hunter level, as a swift action, she can target one foe within 30 feet and designate one willing ally adjacent to that foe as a scapegoat. For the following minute, the target takes a –2 penalty on attacks against any creature other than the designated scapegoat, and the target has a 10% spell failure chance on spells that don't target the scapegoat or include the scapegoat in their area of effect. The penalty increases to –4 at 8th level and –6 at 15th level.

The colluding scoundrel can designate her animal companion as a scapegoat without it counting against her daily uses of this ability.

This is a mind-affecting effect. The effect ends if the colluding scoundrel falls unconscious or is slain.

This replaces animal focus.

Backstabber (Ex): At 8th level, a colluding scoundrel deals 2d6 additional points of damage on attacks against a target threatened by an ally currently designated as the scapegoat. This increases to 3d6 points of damage at 15th level.

This is precision damage and is not multiplied on a critical hit, but it does stack with sneak attack and similar effects.

This replaces second animal focus.

Master Backstabber (Ex): At 20th level, a colluding scoundrel is a master at dispatching distracted targets. As a standard action, she can make a single attack against a foe that is taking the penalties of her scapegoat ability and is adjacent to an ally currently designated as the scapegoat. If the attack hits, the target takes damage normally and must succeed at a Fortitude saving throw (DC = 10 + half the colluding scoundrel's level + her Wisdom modifier) or be slain. Whether or not the target succeeds, it cannot be targeted by this ability again (by any colluding scoundrel) for 24 hours.

This replaces master hunter.

Fallen Heroes

Any path with borders can be strayed from, and characters of classes with alignment or behavioral restrictions (including barbarian, cleric, druid, inquisitor, monk, paladin, and warpriest) sometimes fall out of favor from those classes. Whether by actively embracing forbidden pleasures or a slow departure from their original training, characters who defy the restrictions upon their classes become ex-members of that class.

Typically, an ex-member of a class loses some or even all class features, including animal companions, spellcasting, and other abilities, but not the weapon and armor proficiencies, base attack bonus, or base saving throw bonuses. She cannot gain further levels in that class unless she amends her ways and benefits from an *atonement* spell. But not all characters repent their misdeeds. Some ex-members rage and resent the loss of their abilities, blaming gods or other individuals for their fall; others withdraw into themselves and endure their losses in silent defeat. Still others strive to make up for their losses by taking levels in a new class, working to overcome their failings (or the unfair blow the world has dealt to them, depending on their perspective). A few, however, embrace their fall, gaining new power from the very thing that barred them from the class they once held.

EX-CLASS ARCHETYPES

The following archetypes can be taken by an ex-member of the indicated class immediately upon becoming an ex-member of that class, regardless of character level, replacing some or all of the lost class abilities. If another archetype the character had before she became an ex-member of her class replaces the same ability as the ex-class archetype, she loses the old archetype in favor of the new one; otherwise, she can retain both archetypes as normal. Ex-members of a class with one of the archetypes presented below can gain further levels in the class, even though becoming an ex-member of a class normally prohibits further advancement in the class.

While an ex-member of a class can recant her failings and atone for her fall from her original class (typically involving an *atonement* spell), her acceptance of her ex-class archetype means she must atone both for her initial fall and for further straying from the path. As a result, such a character must be the target of two *atonement* spells or a similar effect to regain her lost class features. Upon doing so, she immediately loses this archetype and regains her original class (and archetype, if she had one).

CHANNELER OF THE UNKNOWN (EX-CLERIC ARCHETYPE)

While most clerics who fall out of favor with their deities simply lose their divine connection and the powers it granted, a few continue to go through the motions of prayer and obedience, persisting in the habits of faith even when their faith itself has faded. Among these, an even smaller number find that while their original deity no longer answers their prayers, something else does: an unknown entity or force of the universe channeling its power through a trained and practicing vessel.

This is an ex-class archetype and can be taken by a character immediately upon becoming an ex-cleric.

Weapon and Armor Proficiency: A channeler of the unknown loses proficiency with her deity's favored weapon. She instead gains proficiency with one martial or exotic weapon, chosen when she first takes this archetype, which thereafter effectively functions as her holy or unholy symbol for the purposes of class abilities and spellcasting. The weapon chosen cannot be one associated with her former deity. Once she makes this choice, she can't later change it.

This alters the cleric's weapon and armor proficiency.

Spells: A channeler of the unknown has one fewer spell slot per spell level in which she can prepare spells than normal. She is no longer restricted by alignment descriptors, and she gains access to all spells on the cleric spell list, even spells her alignment would normally prohibit.

This alters the cleric's spells.

Unknown Aura (Su): A channeler of the unknown never radiates an alignment aura, as if under the effect of a permanent *undetectable alignment* spell.

This replaces the cleric's aura.

Channel Entropy (Su): A channeler of the unknown can channel entropy as a cleric channels negative or positive energy, releasing a wave of twisting void that harms creatures in the area of effect. The amount of damage dealt is equal to that an evil cleric of her level would deal by channeling negative energy, except it affects living, unliving, and undead creatures alike. This functions in all other ways as a cleric's channel energy class feature, including benefiting from feats that affect channel energy (such as Selective Channeling).

This alters channel energy.

Power of the Unknown: A channeler of the unknown has lost the benefit of the domains granted by her deity, but the unknown entity that answers her supplications instead grants her the benefits of one domain from the following list: Darkness, Destruction, Luck, Madness, or Void. Instead of a single domain spell slot, the channeler of the unknown gains two domain spell slots per spell level she can cast. A channeler of the unknown cannot select a subdomain in place of the domain available to her.

This alters the cleric's domains.

Spontaneous Casting: Instead of converting prepared spells into cure or inflict spells, a channeler of the unknown can channel stored spell energy into her domain spells. She can lose a prepared spell, including a domain spell, to spontaneously cast a domain spell of the same spell level or lower.

This alters spontaneous casting.

PLANAR EXTREMIST (EX-DRUID ARCHETYPE)

Through determined interest or repeated exposure to those places where the borders between planes are weaker, some druids lose their neutral stance and find themselves gravitating toward one of the four most extreme alignments: chaotic evil, chaotic good, lawful evil, or lawful good. While no longer able to harness the forces of nature like their neutral kin, these planar extremists find that their powers have shifted to reflect the Outer Plane most closely associated with their alignment.

This is an ex-class archetype and can be taken by a character immediately upon becoming an ex-druid.

Alignment: A planar extremist must have an alignment of chaotic evil, chaotic good, lawful evil, or lawful good.

This alters the druid's alignment.

Aura (Ex): The planar extremist radiates an aura matching her alignment as if she were a cleric of her druid level.

Spells: A planar extremist gains one fewer spell slot per spell level than normal in which to prepare spells. The planar extremist removes all *summon nature's ally* spells from her spell list and replaces them with the *summon monster* spells of the same levels. The druid can otherwise cast spells as normal for a druid of her level.

This alters the druid's spells.

Planar Bond: A planar extremist forms a bond with a manifestation of the Outer Plane with which she is aligned. This bond can take one of two forms. The first is a close tie to the plane to which she is aligned, granting the planar extremist one of the domains of her alignment (for example, a lawful good planar extremist could take either the Lawful or Good domain). This option otherwise functions as a druid's nature bond if she chose a close tie to the natural world.

The second option is to form a close bond with an outsider from an Outer Plane. The abilities of this outsider companion are determined using the rules for eidolons for the unchained summoner[PU] class, as if the planar extremist were a summoner of her druid level, except the outsider companion gains no additional evolution pool (only the evolutions from its base form and base evolutions for its subtype), and it must be of a subtype whose alignment exactly matches the alignment of the planar extremist. The planar extremist can summon her outsider companion with the same 1-minute ritual a summoner normally uses to do so, but she can't cast *summon monster* spells if she currently has her outsider companion summoned, and she can't summon her companion if she already has a creature summoned through other means.

As the planar ally gains class levels, her eidolon's base statistics and base evolutions increase as if her druid level were her summoner level. The eidolon gains the darkvision, link, share spells, evasion, ability score increase, devotion, multiattack, and improved evasion abilities at the appropriate levels, but never gains an evolution pool. Abilities and spells that grant additional evolution points to eidolons do not function for her outsider companion, though any abilities that would grant evolution points to an animal companion do work. The planar extremist does not gain life link or any other class features a summoner gains in relation to her eidolon.

This replaces nature's bond.

Spontaneous Casting: A planar extremist can channel stored spell energy into summoning spells that she hasn't prepared ahead of time. She can lose a prepared spell in order to cast a *summon monster* spell of the same level or lower, but only to summon creatures whose alignment matches hers.

This alters a druid's spontaneous casting.

Resist the Opposite (Ex): At 4th level, a planar extremist gains a +2 bonus on saving throws against the spell-like and supernatural abilities of creatures whose alignment is diametrically opposed to her own.

This replaces resist nature's lure.

Planar Aspect (Su): At 4th level, as a standard action, a planar extremist can gain the benefits of the bloodrager

bloodline associated with her alignment (choosing from Abyssal, Celestial, or Infernal), as if she were a bloodrager of her druid level. She can gain these benefits for 1 minute per druid level as if she were bloodraging (but she gains no other benefits or penalties of bloodrage) or until she dismisses it as a swift action; this duration need not be used consecutively but must be spent in 1-minute increments. She can use this ability an additional time per day at 6th level and every 4 levels thereafter, for a total of five times per day at 18th level. At 20th level, a planar extremist can use planar aspect at will.

This replaces wild shape.

Sin Monk (Ex-Monk Archetype)

Some vices prove too tempting even to those who have trained their minds and bodies against such corruptions, and the seven sins of ancient Thassilon stand among the most alluring. Martial experts who have allowed such passions to lead them astray may find themselves gaining powers drawn from their newly embraced sins.

This is an ex-class archetype and can be taken by a character immediately upon becoming an ex-monk.

Well of Sin (Su): At 4th level, a sin monk gains a pool of sin points, representing energy he has gained from indulging in forbidden vices. The sin monk has a number of sin points equal to half his class level + his Wisdom modifier; these points cannot be used on abilities that require spending ki points. As a swift action, he can spend 1 point from his sin pool to activate one of the following abilities until the start of his next turn.

Envy: The sin monk gains a +4 bonus on Perception and Sense Motive checks. This bonus increases to +6 at 10th level and +8 at 16th level.

Gluttony: Each time the sin monk deals lethal damage with a melee attack, he regains a number of hit points equal to the amount of damage dealt (maximum 2). He can't exceed his maximum number of hit points. The maximum number of hit points he regains increases to 4 at 10th level and 6 at 16th level.

Greed: The sin monk's attacks count as being either cold iron or silver (sin monk's choice) for the purpose of overcoming DR. At 10th level, he adds adamantine to the list of materials he can choose to have his attacks count as being for the purpose of overcoming DR. At 16th level, the sin monk's attacks also ignore hardness.

Lust: The sin monk gains a +4 bonus on Bluff and Diplomacy checks. This bonus increases to +6 at 10th level and +8 at 16th level.

Pride: The sin monk gains one illusory double of himself, which functions as *mirror image*. This double automatically disappears at the beginning of the sin monk's next turn unless destroyed first. At 10th level, the sin monk gains two such replicas of himself, and at 16th level, he gains three.

Sloth: The sin monk gains the benefits of Vital Strike. At 10th level, he also gains the benefits of Improved Vital Strike, and at 16th level, he also gains the benefits of Greater Vital Strike.

Wrath: The sin monk increases the save DCs of his attacks with Stunning Fist (and Punishing Kick, if he has that feat) by 1. The save DC instead increases by 2 at 10th level and by 3 at 16th level.

When a sin monk gains a level in the monk class and would gain one of the following class features, he can forfeit that class feature to instead increase the size of his sin pool by 1 sin point: purity of body, diamond body, diamond soul, timeless body, tongue of the sun and moon. Once the decision is made, it cannot be changed.

This replaces ki pool and alters high jump.

Sinful Strike (Su): At 7th level, a sin monk can spend 2 sin points as a swift action to focus his power. The next time he deals damage before the end of his next turn, he deals an additional amount damage equal to his monk level.

This replaces wholeness of body.

Burden with Sin (Su): At 12th level, a sin monk can spend a swift action and one daily use of Stunning Fist to draw his sinful nature to the fore of his consciousness. The next person he hits with a melee attack before the end of his next turn must succeed at a Will save (DC = 10 + half the sin monk's class level + his Wisdom modifier) or suffer the burden of the sin monk's sins. The target is treated as if she were carrying a load one step heavier (from a light load to a medium load, and so on) and must succeed at a caster level check to use any form of teleportation (DC = 10 + the monk's class level). This is a curse^UM effect that lasts a number of rounds equal to the sin monk's Wisdom modifier unless it is removed through *remove curse* or a similar effect.

This replaces abundant step.

Simultaneous Sins (Su): At 19th level, a sin monk can spend 3 points from his sin pool as a swift action to gain the benefits of two different sins simultaneously.

This replaces empty body.

Spawn of Sin (Ex): At 20th level, the sin monk becomes the physical manifestation of his sins. He is forevermore treated as an aberration rather than a humanoid (or whatever the monk's creature type was) for the purpose of spells and magical effects, and his mind is so consumed by sin that he gains immunity to mind-affecting effects. He does not change in appearance or gain other abilities; however, should the sin monk be slain and brought back from the dead, he returns to life as a sinspawn (*Pathfinder RPG Bestiary* 2 246), retaining his class levels but otherwise replacing his creature type and racial abilities with those of his new form and becoming an NPC under the GM's control.

This replaces perfect self.

Vindictive Bastard (Ex-Paladin Archetype)

While paladins often collaborate with less righteous adventurers in order to further their causes, those who spend too much time around companions with particularly loose morals run the risk of adopting those same unscrupulous ideologies and methods. Such a vindictive bastard, as these fallen paladins are known, strikes out for retribution and revenge, far more interested in tearing down those who have harmed her or her companions than furthering a distant deity's cause.

This is an ex-class archetype and can be taken by a character immediately upon becoming an ex-paladin.

No Aura: A vindictive bastard does not radiate an alignment aura.

This alters the paladin's aura.

Locate Ally (Sp): Once per day, a vindictive bastard can cast *locate creature* as a spell-like ability with a caster level equal to her paladin level, but she can do so only to target an ally whom she has spent at least 24 hours in close proximity to within the last week. This replaces detect evil.

Vindictive Smite (Ex): A vindictive bastard is particularly ruthless against those who have harmed her or her allies. Once per day as a swift action, she can smite one target within sight who has dealt hit point damage to her or an ally. She adds her Charisma modifier to her attack rolls and adds her paladin level to damage rolls against the target of her smite. In addition, while vindictive smite is in effect, the vindictive bastard gains a deflection bonus equal to her Charisma bonus (if any) to her AC against attacks by the target of the smite. If the target of vindictive smite has rendered an ally of the vindictive bastard unconscious or dead within the last 24 hours, the bonus on damage rolls on the first attack that hits increases by 2 for every paladin level she has.

The vindictive smite effect remains until the target of the smite is dead or the next time the vindictive bastard rests and regains her uses of this ability. At 4th level and every 3 levels thereafter, the vindictive bastard can invoke her vindictive smite one additional time per day, to a maximum of seven times per day at 19th level.

This replaces smite evil.

Faded Grace (Ex): At 2nd level, a vindictive bastard gains one of the following as a bonus feat: Great Fortitude, Iron Will, or Lightning Reflexes.

This replaces divine grace.

Solo Tactics (Ex): At 2nd level, a vindictive bastard gains solo tactics, as per the inquisitor class feature. She can activate this ability as a swift action and gains the benefits of it for 1 round. She can use this ability a number of rounds per day equal to half her paladin level + her Charisma modifier.

This replaces lay on hands.

Spiteful Tenacity (Ex): At 3rd level, whenever a vindictive bastard has a vindictive smite in effect, she gains the benefits of the Diehard feat.

This replaces divine health.

Teamwork Feat: At 3rd level and every 6 levels thereafter, the vindictive bastard gains a bonus feat in addition to those gained from normal advancement. These bonus feats must be selected from those listed as teamwork feats. The vindictive bastard must meet the prerequisites of the selected bonus feat.

This replaces mercy and channel energy.

Gang Up (Ex): At 5th level, a vindictive bastard forms a close bond with her companions. This allows her to spend a move action to grant half her vindictive smite bonus against a single target to all allies within 30 feet who can see and hear her. This bonus lasts for a number of rounds equal to the vindictive bastard's Charisma modifier (minimum 1).

This replaces divine bond.

Swift Justice (Ex): At 11th level, a vindictive bastard can activate her gang up ability as a swift action.

This replaces aura of justice.

Stalwart (Ex): At 14th level, a vindictive bastard gains stalwart, as per the inquisitor class feature, except she can also benefit from this ability while wearing heavy armor.

This replaces aura of faith.

Aura of Self-Righteousness (Ex): At 17th level, a vindictive bastard gains DR 5/lawful or good and immunity to compulsion spells and spell-like abilities. Each ally within 10 feet of her gains a +4 morale bonus on saving throws against compulsion effects. Aura of self-righteousness functions only while the vindictive bastard is conscious, not if she is unconscious or dead.

This replaces aura of righteousness.

Ultimate Vindication (Ex): At 20th level, if a foe kills one of a vindictive bastard's allies or knocks the vindictive bastard unconscious (and she later regains consciousness), the vindictive bastard musters a vindictive fury. The next time she hits that foe within 1 minute, the vindictive bastard can channel the effects of a *disintegrate* spell through her weapon, using her paladin level as her effective caster level. Whether or not the target succeeds at its save against the *disintegrate* effect, it is immune to this ability for the next 24 hours.

This replaces holy champion.

Antiheroes are often adaptive, multitalented, and more than capable of surviving on their own, so it is no surprise that many choose the path of the vigilante. While most characters are restricted to nine alignment options, vigilantes' dual identity class feature allows them to combine two alignments, resulting in a much greater number of alignment options for each individual.

The darker, more antisocial side of an antiheroic vigilante's personality can just as easily be his true nature or a facade, and it might serve as his social identity or his vigilante identity. For instance, a respected philanthropist may turn into a ruthless avenger after nightfall, or he might be a callous thief who makes donations as a ruse to turn attention away from the lavish lifestyle he maintains at others' expense. Conversely, a young aristocrat who is seemingly squandering her inheritance may in truth be a dedicated defender of the common people.

SOCIAL TALENTS

The following social talents allow antiheroes and outcasts to better blend in with polite society.

Beginner's Luck (Ex): The vigilante appears so harmless and innocent that onlookers dismiss his incredible abilities as nothing more than beginner's luck. When the vigilante uses a vigilante talent while in his social identity, he can add the +20 circumstance bonus from seamless guise to his Disguise check to fool onlookers, so long as the number of onlookers witnessing him is no greater than his vigilante level. The vigilante's PC allies do not count as onlookers (and at the GM's discretion, a closely allied NPC might not count as an onlooker, either). He loses this bonus against onlookers who have already witnessed him using a vigilante talent in his social identity within the last week.

Conflicted Identity (Ex): The vigilante's mind is in a constant state of turmoil, which makes him even more ethically and morally fluid than other vigilantes. When targeted by a harmful spell or effect that would affect the vigilante in his current identity but not his other identity (or when he would suffer a lesser effect in his other identity), he has a 50% chance of being affected as though he were in his other identity. This chance is rolled when the spell or effect is cast or triggered and before any spell resistance roll, if applicable. For example, if a vigilante has a lawful-neutral social identity and a neutral vigilante identity, he has a 50% chance of taking only half damage from a *chaos hammer* spell while in his social identity, since he would always take only half damage from a *chaos hammer* spell when in his vigilante identity.

Hidden Magic (Ex): The auras of magic items the vigilante is carrying are hidden (as per *magic aura*). The vigilante can suppress or reactivate this effect as a standard action. At 11th level, the vigilante and any magic items he is carrying appear to be nonmagical (as if he had cast *greater magic aura*). The vigilante must be at least 5th level to select this talent.

Notorious Fool (Ex): While in his social identity, the vigilante can feign absentmindedness, clumsiness, drunkenness, or eccentricity very convincingly. When he fails an opposed Sleight of Hand or Stealth check while in his social identity, he can immediately attempt a Bluff check opposed by the onlookers' Sense Motive checks to appear as though he had only blundered or stumbled in a spectacular fashion. If he succeeds at this Bluff check, the onlookers do not realize the vigilante was attempting the action that prompted him to attempt a Sleight of Hand or Stealth check, although being in the wrong place or behaving in an inappropriate manner may still have negative consequences. This talent is ineffective against any onlooker who has already witnessed the vigilante faking a blunder within the last 24 hours.

VIGILANTE TALENTS

The following vigilante talents include techniques favored by unscrupulous heroes who are willing to do almost anything to save the day.

Combat Expertise (Ex): The vigilante gains Combat Expertise as a bonus feat, even if he doesn't meet the prerequisites. If he already has Combat Expertise, he instead gains another feat he qualified for at the level when he chose Combat Expertise. If the vigilante's Intelligence score is less than 13, it counts as 13 for the purpose of meeting the prerequisites of combat feats.

Poisoner (Ex): The vigilante gains the alchemist's poison use class feature. At 6th level, when he has 5 doses of a single kind of poison, he can synthesize a dose of that poison once per day at no cost. This process takes 1 minute. It doesn't expend the 5 doses of poison, but the doses must be in the vigilante's possession to perform the synthesis. The poison produced requires careful storage and special skill to use. It becomes inert if it leaves the vigilante's possession and can't be sold. The vigilante can maintain only 1 dose of synthesized poison for every 5 doses of that poison in his possession.

Signature Arrows (Ex): The vigilante must select one type of bow or crossbow (such as shortbow or heavy crossbow) when he selects this talent. After the first time the vigilante buys a set of 50 pieces of magic ammunition intended for that type of bow or crossbow, he can pay the construction cost instead of the purchase price for additional ammunition with identical magical effects for the same weapon, even if he could not normally craft magic ammunition. This benefit applies only to the first type of magic ammunition that the vigilante buys 50 pieces of for the designated weapon. The vigilante can take this talent more than once; each time he takes it, he can purchase and gain this benefit with either a specific type of magic ammunition for a different type of bow or crossbow or a different type of magic ammunition for the original weapon. The vigilante must be at least 14th level to select this talent.

Sweeping Strike (Ex): The vigilante gains Cleave as a bonus feat. At 6th level, he gains Great Cleave as a bonus feat.

He does not need to meet the prerequisites for these feats. At 12th level, while using Great Cleave, he no longer has to hit a target in order to make an additional attack against a foe that is adjacent to that target. Only an avenger vigilante can select this talent.

Vigilante's Reflexes (Ex): The vigilante gains Combat Reflexes as a bonus feat. If he already has the Combat Reflexes feat, he instead gains another feat he qualified for at the level when he chose Combat Reflexes. At 8th and 16th levels, the number of additional attacks of opportunity per round the vigilante can make increases by 1, regardless of the vigilante's Dexterity bonus.

SPLINTERSOUL
(VIGILANTE ARCHETYPE)

A splintersoul pushes the boundaries of what it means to have two separate identities. One may be kind and calm while the other is angry and heartless, and the change from one identity to another is sudden and frightening. The splintersoul is torn by conflicting emotions and thoughts, but because of his dual mind, he can master a uniquely disparate set of skills and abilities no normal person should be able to manage.

Splintered Identity (Ex): A splintersoul's two identities are even more distant from one another than those of a normal vigilante. He cannot use any of his vigilante talents while in his social identity.

However, for the purpose of qualifying for classes, feats, and other abilities, he is eligible if one of his alignments meets the requirements. While in an identity whose alignment is incompatible with an ability, class, or feat, he temporarily loses access to the feat or ability or is treated as an ex-member of the class, as appropriate.

For example, a splintersoul with barbarian levels, a lawful-good social identity, and a neutral vigilante identity can't use his vigilante talents or his rage class feature while in his social identity, but he regains these abilities and can use them as normal as soon as he changes to his vigilante identity.

A splintersoul with paladin levels must follow the paladin's normal code of conduct while in a lawful-good identity, but while in an identity with a different alignment, the following changes apply to his code: Willingly committing an evil act (for example, casting a spell with the evil descriptor) still causes the vigilante to become an ex-paladin, but otherwise, he can do whatever else he feels is necessary to uphold the causes of law and good. He should strive to act with honor and uphold the tenets of his faith, but failing to do so is not a violation of his code. At the GM's discretion, other classes or archetypes with similarly strict codes of conduct can also follow a less strict version of a code of conduct while in an identity with an incompatible alignment.

This alters dual identity.

Sudden Change (Ex): More adaptive than other vigilantes, a splintersoul must select the quick change social talent at 3rd level and the immediate change social talent at 7th level, ignoring the minimum levels for those talents.

This replaces unshakable and alters the social talents gained at 3rd and 7th levels.

Surprising Change (Ex): At 7th level, when a splintersoul uses the immediate change talent to reveal his vigilante identity and then attacks a foe in the same round, he can use the startling appearance ability against that foe as though the foe were unaware of his presence. At 11th and 17th levels, he can use frightening appearance and stunning appearance, respectively, while using this ability. A splintersoul can use frightening appearance and stunning appearance only against foes who are unaware of his presence, and he can do so a number of times per day equal to his Charisma modifier. This ability doesn't function against foes who already know the splintersoul's identity.

This alters startling appearance, frightening appearance, and stunning appearance.

Cost of Sacrifice

The lives of many adventurers involve a great deal of grievous injury, hardship, personal sacrifice, or a smattering of all three. For most heroes, these losses are painful but necessary setbacks in the pursuit of their noble goals and causes. Many antiheroes, however, have a past that is so riddled with guilt, loss, and pain that they end up abandoning the pursuit of personal happiness. Instead, these antiheroes become mired in the losses they have suffered. They become broken, jaded, or empty versions of their former selves as resentment settles into their psyches—resentment for what could have been, what was stolen from them, or what sacrifices were forced upon them.

For most such antiheroes, this burden is deeply emotional. A fighter may take great risks for an ally who reminds her of the sister she failed to protect in her youth, though she might never go to such lengths for others. A wizard may go by himself to confront the evil creatures he unleashed in a self-serving experiment gone terribly wrong. A former noble might become a monk with an enormous chip on her shoulder after a decision made by a privileged peer with a callous disregard for the common people led to a terrible tragedy.

While these often self-imposed burdens weigh heavily on any antiheroes who carry them, a select few are able to harness the effects of their pain and suffering in a way that supernaturally manifests their grief in the heat of battle, forcing their enemies to confront the agony the antiheroes live with each day.

Other antiheroes are born into a bloodline that overflows with an ancestor's purposeful suffering; a forebear may have laid down his life for a noble cause or paid the ultimate price in a final act of defiance. An antihero with such an ancestor can draw great power from that fount, channeling the sorrow of their familial past into great physical prowess. Still other antiheroes find unique ways to shape the great sacrifices they've made and the losses they've felt into power that helps them achieve their own myriad goals.

PHANTOM EMOTIONAL FOCUS

The following new emotional focus is available to spiritualists (*Pathfinder RPG Occult Adventures* 72) whose phantoms suffered greatly in life, usually as a cost of pursuing a powerful ideal or defending a loved one—sometimes even the spiritualist herself.

SUFFERING

Phantoms with this focus stand on trembling legs, with hands quivering and tears constantly streaming from their eyes. Their auras are typically a blue or purple, but the phantoms have vividly glowing scars and bruises that pulse and throb with their motion. When addressed, they tend to respond with only slight nods and other subtle gestures, rarely speaking beyond soft-spoken apologies and self-recriminations. While clearly in a state of constant pain, they show no concern for their own well-being, focusing entirely on protecting their masters and their masters' allies. Each time one of these phantoms uses its abilities to protect its allies from harm, new injuries manifest visibly upon it, which these phantoms wear like badges of honor.

Skills: The phantom gains a number of ranks in Climb and Heal equal to its number of Hit Dice. When confined in the spiritualist's consciousness, the phantom grants the spiritualist Skill Focus in each of these skills.

Good Saves: Fortitude and Will.

Endurance: The phantom gains Endurance as a bonus feat. Furthermore, when the phantom is confined in its master's consciousness, it grants the benefits of Endurance to its master if its master doesn't have that feat.

Repelling Strike (Ex): When the phantom deals damage with a melee attack, it can attempt to bull rush the target as a swift action without provoking attacks of opportunity, using the result of its attack roll for the combat maneuver check. The phantom can push a creature back only 5 feet with this ability, regardless of the result of its combat maneuver check.

Numbing Aura (Su): When the spiritualist reaches 7th level, as a swift action, the phantom can emit a 20-foot aura of protection. Allies within this aura gain a +4 bonus on saving throws against curse, disease, evil,

fear, pain, and poison effects (*Pathfinder RPG Ultimate Magic* 137–138). Deactivating the aura is a free action. The phantom can use this ability in either ectoplasmic or incorporeal form.

Suffer in Stead (Su): When the spiritualist reaches 12th level, as an immediate action when her phantom is fully manifested and within 30 feet of her, she can transfer any of the following conditions to the phantom that would afflict her: blinded, deafened, exhausted, fatigued, nauseated, paralyzed, sickened, staggered, or stunned. The spiritualist must choose to do this before the condition's duration begins. The spiritualist can't use this ability if any of the listed conditions are already affecting the phantom. Using this ability does not affect the duration of the transferred condition; it simply makes the condition affect the phantom instead of the spiritualist.

When the spiritualist reaches 18th level, as an immediate action when fully manifested, the phantom can use this ability to transfer any of the listed conditions to itself when the condition would afflict any ally within 30 feet. Using the ability in this way requires no additional action from the spiritualist.

Willing Martyr (Su): When the spiritualist reaches 17th level, the phantom begins to anticipate when the spiritualist or her allies would fall into grave bodily danger and can take those wounds itself. Whenever the phantom is fully manifested and the spiritualist or an ally is reduced to one-quarter or fewer hit points, as long as the phantom is within 30 feet, it must take any hit point damage or ability score damage in place of the injured spiritualist or ally. This hit point damage or ability score damage bypasses the phantom's defensive abilities (although it is still subject to the defensive abilities of the originally targeted spiritualist or ally) and afflicts the phantom as it would the spiritualist or ally. After the phantom becomes the target of one attack or effect in place of the injured spiritualist or ally, the spiritualist can command the phantom to suppress this ability as a free action. Reactivating this ability is a swift action.

BLOODRAGER BLOODLINE

The following new bloodline is available to bloodragers (*Pathfinder RPG Advanced Class Guide* 15). Bloodragers who want to take levels in sorcerer (or sorcerers who want to take levels in bloodrager) should make note of the martyred sorcerer bloodline that can be found on page 29 of *Pathfinder Player Companion: Blood of Angels*.

Martyred

One of your ancestors paid the ultimate price for her beliefs. This distant relative martyred herself out of a devout dedication to some specific cause, and that sacrifice has infused you with power that you can use for good—or for ill. When you bloodrage, an inspiring fury conjures echoes of your forebear's incredible determination and selfless dedication, both offering you protection and amplifying your ability to punish any who dare incur your wrath.

Bonus Feats: Diehard, Endurance, Heroic Defiance[APG], Heroic Recovery[APG], Leadership, Persuasive, Toughness.

Bonus Spells: *Endure elements* (7th), *surmount affliction*[UM] (10th), *heroism* (13th), *blessing of fervor*[APG] (16th).

Bloodline Powers: When you bloodrage, you channel the power of your ancestor's self-sacrifice to urge yourself and your allies on to greater feats of strength than would otherwise be possible.

Ancestral Strikes (Su): At 1st level, three times per day as a swift action, you can imbue your melee attacks with a measure of your ancestor's power. For 1 round, your melee attacks deal 1d6 additional points of good-aligned damage if you are good, or they deal 1d6 additional points of evil-aligned damage if you are evil. If you are neutral, you must choose which type of damage this ability deals when you choose this bloodline, and the decision cannot be changed later. At 8th level, you can use this ability up to five times per day. At 20th level, all your melee attacks deal this additional damage, and you don't need to activate this ability.

Martyr's Resistances (Su): At 4th level, you gain fire resistance 5 and you gain a +2 bonus on saving throws against fear and pain effects (*Ultimate Magic* 138). At 8th level, your fire resistance increases to 10, and the bonus on saving throws against fear and pain effects increases to +4.

Forebear's Reserves (Su): At 8th level, you can reroll a saving throw once during a bloodrage. You must decide to use this ability after the die is rolled but before the GM reveals the result. You must take the second result, even if it's worse.

Ancestral Champion (Su): At 12th level, when your ancestral strikes target a creature whose alignment is opposite to the type of damage the strikes deal, your ancestral strikes instead deal 2d6 additional 2d6 points of damage of that type.

Sacrificial Exchange (Su): At 16th level, as a swift action once per day while you are bloodraging, you can take a –2 penalty to Armor Class to grant one ally within 30 feet a +4 morale bonus to one ability score. (This penalty to your AC stacks with the penalty from your bloodrage.) The penalty and bonus last for the duration of your bloodrage. At 20th level, the penalty this ability imposes changes to –4, and the ally's bonus increases to +6.

Eternal Martyr (Su): Your ancestor's sacrifice transcends time and space, keeping you alive when you otherwise shouldn't be and sanctifying your form. At 20th level, your ancestor's act of martyrdom infuses your spirit. You become immune to death effects. Material components for spells and effects to bring you back to life (such as *raise dead* or *resurrection*) cost half as much as normal. Your body cannot be turned into an undead creature, as though you were affected by a permanent *hallow* effect (caster level = your bloodrager level). You have these benefits constantly, even while not bloodraging.

Amoral Corruption

While even the noblest heroes can fall victim to corruption of body, mind, or spirit, antiheroes who tread ethically gray waters are often at higher risk of losing themselves to the moral decay detailed below. Full rules for corruption can be found starting on page 14 of *Pathfinder RPG Horror Adventures*.

When an otherwise upstanding person turns to evil deeds to achieve his goals—whether by accident, due to sinister influence, or through desperation—he begins to slip, every excuse and justification furthering his descent into evil.

CATALYST

This corruption often begins when you allow an evil force into your life to help you accomplish an otherwise noble goal. In the name of helping a community or saving a loved one, you may have fallen in league with a disguised succubus or made a desperate deal with a dark power.

Characters who are already neutral or evil cannot gain this corruption.

PROGRESSION

The progression of this corruption is tied to evil actions taken to achieve a significant benevolent goal (identified when you gain this corruption), especially when such actions provide an easier road to success than good actions. A significant goal might be deposing a tyrant or rescuing a prisoner of war, but it is up to the GM to determine what qualifies. Whenever you commit an evil act in pursuit of your significant goal, you must attempt a Will saving throw (DC = 15 + your manifestation level). You must also attempt this saving throw after any month in which the number of evil acts you performed in pursuit of your goal is less than your manifestation level. If you fail any of these saving throws, you are overcome with the urge to commit a wantonly evil act that does not significantly advance your benevolent goal; this also causes you to progress to the next corruption stage. If others prevent this wantonly evil act, you shake off this urge, but the DC of future saving throws to prevent the corruption's progress increases by 2; this increase stacks each time you shake off the urge, but it resets when you reach the next corruption stage.

Performing a wantonly evil action for your own enjoyment automatically progresses the corruption to the next stage.

Corruption Stage 1: The first time you engage in an evil act to further your goal, your alignment shifts one step toward evil.

Corruption Stage 2: The second time you engage in such an act, your alignment shifts another step toward evil, you take on a sickly pallor, and your pupils turn dark red.

Corruption Stage 3: The third time you engage in such an act, evil behavior becomes a casual part of your actions and you think nothing of the suffering caused to bring about your goals—after all, it will be worth it. However, you might lose sight of your original purpose in favor of mean-spiritedness. You become an NPC under the GM's control.

REMOVING THE CORRUPTION

This corruption is difficult to remove, since it is based in part on your self-delusions. You must first be convinced that you are going too far to achieve your goal, and even then, full recovery requires atoning (as per *atonement*) or going through a similar redemptive arc, with the potential of remission subject to the GM's discretion.

MANIFESTATIONS

The following are manifestations of the amoral corruption. Prerequisites marked with an asterisk (*) appear in this section.

CLANDESTINE DEALINGS

You begin to see the value in the methods of your enemies, and this intrigues them.

Gift: When you attempt a Diplomacy check to influence the attitude of an unfriendly or hostile creature, the DC is reduced by 5.

Stain: The hypocrisy of your methods begins to catch up with you. Good-aligned weapons and damaging effects deal one additional die of damage to you, even if your current alignment is good. (For example, a +1 *holy longsword* deals 2d8+1 points of damage to you if you are not evil, and it deals 2d8+2d6+1 points of damage to you if you are evil.)

Evidence Eraser

You fear discovery of your crimes, so you work with obsessive zeal to cover your tracks, though this makes you paranoid.

Gift: You gain a +4 profane bonus on Bluff checks to obscure or destroy evidence, as well as on Stealth checks. At manifestation level 3rd, this bonus becomes +8.

Stain: You constantly second-guess the motives of others. If you attempt a Sense Motive check against a character who is not being deceptive, you must succeed against a DC equal to 15 + your manifestation level or you form some outlandish theory about the character's behavior that paints her as an obstacle to accomplishing your goal.

Evidence Forger

You don't care about truth; you care only that the "facts" support your agenda, and you are adept at making such falsehoods seem true.

Prerequisites: Manifestation level 3rd, evidence eraser*.

Gift: When attempting a Linguistics or similar check to create a forged piece of evidence, you can roll twice and use the higher result. You can use this gift a number of times per week equal to your manifestation level.

Stain: You can no longer discern between reality and a plausible lie. Whenever you attempt either a Will saving throw to disbelieve an illusion or an opposed Sense Motive check, you roll twice and take the lower result.

Forbidden Magic

You find your magic to be insufficient for reaching your goal, so you begin to draw from darker sources.

Prerequisite: Manifestation level 3rd.

Gift: When you are the target of a damaging or healing spell, before the damage or healing is rolled, you can choose to take one fewer die of damage (for a damaging spell) or add one die of healing (for a healing spell).

Stain: Each time you use forbidden magic's gift, you must succeed at a Will saving throw (DC = 15 + your manifestation level) or you progress to the next corruption stage.

Greater Clandestine Dealings

Fiends have taken notice of your wavering beliefs, and they seek to entice you.

Prerequisites: Manifestation level 3rd, clandestine dealings*.

Gift: The benefits of clandestine dealings also apply to evil outsiders, regardless of their initial attitude. Furthermore, such outsiders are always willing to offer bargains, whether they are encountered normally or called by *planar binding* or similar methods.

Stain: You count as evil for the purposes of spells that have alignment-based effects.

Overwhelming Hate

You cannot abide those who would oppose your goals—the very thought makes your blood boil.

Prerequisite: Manifestation level 6th.

Gift: Once per day, you can declare an enemy to be a threat to your goal, allowing you to add your manifestation level as a bonus on damage rolls against that enemy. At manifestation level 8th, this extra damage is doubled.

Stain: When you encounter a significant setback in reaching your goal (as determined by the GM), you must attempt a Will saving throw (DC = 15 + your manifestation level). On a failure, you attempt to take revenge on the party you consider responsible within the next few days, and your corruption progresses to the next stage.

Self-Righteous Fury

Your fury at being vexed knows no bounds, and you sometimes slip into violent rages.

Prerequisite: Manifestation level 6th.

Gift: Three times per day, you can gain the benefits of the *rage* spell with a caster level equal to your manifestation level. At manifestation level 8th, you also gain the benefits of the *haste* spell for as long as your rage lasts.

Stain: Your temper is difficult to control. Whenever you fail an ability check or skill check by 5 or more, you must succeed at a Will saving throw (DC = 15 + your manifestation level) or you immediately lash out at a creature or object involved in the situation (determined randomly if there are multiple targets), attacking it with a weapon or otherwise attempting to damage it. You are not compelled to continue attacking the target.

Sociopathic Liar

You have become so adept at spinning mistruths that it becomes nearly impossible for others to understand your true motives.

Gift: Whenever you attempt a Bluff check to lie, you gain a +4 bonus on the check. At manifestation level 3rd, this bonus increases to +8.

Stain: Whenever you are telling the truth and a creature attempts a Sense Motive check, the creature suspects you are lying regardless of the check's result.

Sudden Betrayal

Your allies never suspect that you will betray them in an instant if they get in your way.

Prerequisite: Manifestation level 6th.

Gift: When you initiate combat against your allies, each one is staggered for the first normal round of combat.

Stain: You don't count other creatures as allies for the purposes of abilities and effects that don't directly target them (excluding the gift of this manifestation).

Antiheroic Organizations

Many organizations across Golarion delve into murky ethical territory. Such organizations prove appealing to those who take a utilitarian view of things, from business magnates who consider the deaths of a few innocents a reasonable price to pay for profit to spies who make moral compromises to avoid detection. Some such groups are neutrally aligned. Others are outright evil, and those who join them in pursuit of worthy goals must take care to avoid sliding into evil. This path requires a difficult balancing act, but some view it as the easiest—or only—way to achieve their aims.

FREE CAPTAINS

More a loose confederation of pirates than a unified organization, the Free Captains of the Shackles are feared throughout the Inner Sea region. These pirates are nominally led by the Pirate Council, a small group of the most powerful Free Captains, headed by the Hurricane King (currently a human man named Kerdak Bonefist). In practice, the council rarely interferes with the pirates within its domain, unless they cross one of the council members or their activities threaten the security of the Free Captains as a whole. The pirates occasionally unify against outside threats, but such alliances usually last only as long as the threat does before the captains return to their own businesses, goals, and rivalries.

There are no set standards for membership; all one needs to declare oneself a Free Captain is a ship and piratical acumen. The Free Captains coordinate raids throughout the Shackles and along the Garundi coast, from Rahadoum to the jungles of Sargava. They have as many goals as there are Free Captains themselves, but they always have in common a love of piracy and a respect for the sea. Many among the Free Captains worship Besmara, the Pirate Queen, and even those who are not devoted specifically to the goddess's service often offer her a prayer before a journey or a battle—after all, it is never wise to offend the mistress of one's environment.

Joining the crew of a Free Captain is a natural fit for many antiheroic characters. Whether a dashing swashbuckler or a sorcerer with the pull of the sea in her veins, just about anyone is welcome upon the Free Captains' ships provided that she's an asset to the crew. Such antiheroic characters may have been raised among pirates from childhood, or they might have joined later to elude an enemy or an awful fate. The freedom given to the Free Captains enables those among their ranks to pursue a wide variety of aims, and their flexible morals allow antiheroic characters a great deal of opportunity and leeway for dubious operations. Antiheroic characters might be devout followers of Besmara, or they may raid merchant ships or act as pirates in order to further the cause of another nation. They might even aim for a seat on the Pirate Council. In the endlessly

shifting web of pirate alliances and rivalries, patrons are easily found and lost, offenses easily committed and redeemed, and opportunity abounds for wealth and notoriety—assuming one does not find a watery grave first.

NINJA CLANS

Little known in the Inner Sea region, the ninja clans of Tian Xia are notorious throughout that region, though seldom discussed publicly—particularly in their birthplace of Minkai. Many of the traditional tales of Minkai about the ninja clans star antiheroes of some sort, whether these figures are working in the shadows for a noble cause or seeking a fortune to better their families' lives. In such tales, the antiheroes of the ninja serve as a counterpoint to the more traditional samurai heroes. Ninja are not restricted to battlefields; rather, these warriors operate in the shadows, whether serving their clan's aims or those of a patron noble family. Primarily feared as assassins and spies, each clan has a different outlook and specialization, and learning a ninja's clan provides many clues about her skills. Such clans maintain their traditions firmly, and members who act against the clan's interests are unlikely to be given a second chance.

While some are born into a clan, many choose to join one for a variety of reasons, whether it's because they support the clan's organizing principles or because they seek to strike against a common enemy. Multiple ninja clans exist throughout Minkai and the rest of Tian Xia, but a few are especially suitable for antiheroic characters. The Emerald Branch, a clan sworn to defend the common people, would appeal to someone dedicated to defending good causes even if it requires bending or breaking the law. The clan's strong opposition to evil dictatorships and tyranny ensures a warm welcome for any who share those goals. An antiheroic character could also find a place among the Dragonshadow clan, which is rumored to serve an imperial dragon. These ninja specialize in subterfuge and theft, seeking out treasure for their mysterious leader, and such activities attract those also hunting for valuable items.

Though the ninja class is a natural fit for a member of the ninja clans of Tian Xia, it is not a strict requirement, and there is plenty of room for additional specializations, depending on the clan involved. Joining a ninja clan provides both opportunity and risk, as members may become embroiled in the political dealings of a patron noble family, a fight against a tyrannical overlord, or a dangerous—but potentially lucrative—treasure hunt.

RED MANTIS

Headquartered on Mediogalti Island off the coast of Rahadoum, the Red Mantis assassins are unique in that they are not merely a group of mercenaries. Though they do carry out assassination jobs in exchange for payment, they also view such killings as a sacred rite dedicated to their patron deity, Achaekek. They will not kill rightful monarchs—though they view usurpers as fair game—and sometimes they turn down a job with no explanation. The Red Mantis are overseen by a ruling council called the Vernai, a group of high-ranking members second in power only to the Blood Mistress. From their Crimson Citadel, the Red Mantis assassins train new members, accept or reject contracts, and keep an eye on those who may require their services.

Though the organization itself is lawful evil, not all of its members are, and an antiheroic character could certainly join their ranks. The Red Mantis are respected and feared, and they have attained a cult status in the city of Ilizmagorti, which they founded as a place where potential clients could seek them out. Antiheroic characters who are in the Red Mantis or hope to join might be Ilizmagorti natives who see the organization as the best way to advance in society, or they might be devotees of Achaekek with a more neutral outlook. To such a follower, the Red Mantis's services are a necessary, if distasteful, part of the multiverse—a sacred obligation misunderstood by most.

An association with the Red Mantis provides power and prestige, but the organization requires its members to act in the service of the Mantis God at all times. This could eventually force an antiheroic character to make a choice between her private goals and those of the Red Mantis, should they happen to conflict. Even so, many would consider the potential benefits well worth the risk, particularly if one is able to stick to assassinations of more "deserving" targets. An antiheroic Red Mantis member might hope to assassinate those who are corrupt or unethical; though the organization does not assassinate legitimate monarchs, this still leaves a wide variety of potential targets. In the course of completing an assassination or gathering information, a character involved with the Red Mantis may become involved in a multitude of activities, from treasure hunts to espionage to political intrigue, particularly if the character is hiding her affiliation.

SCZARNI

A loose association of Varisian crime syndicates composed of individual families and their underlings, the Sczarni are notorious throughout Varisia and beyond. Most other Varisians are not fond of them and are quick to remind outsiders that not all Varisians are Sczarni, as they perpetuate popular stereotypes of Varisians as thieving rascals. Though the Sczarni are often spoken of as a single unified whole, each family is an independent unit, and alliances and rivalries spring up between them with astonishing rapidity. The Sczarni are infamous for pickpocketing, robbery, and con games perpetuated upon unsuspecting marks. They typically eschew violent crimes, though many families pay specialized executioners to do their rougher jobs, if required.

This focus on trickery over violence has caused an almost romantic narrative to spring up around the Sczarni in some places, with ballads and tales praising the Sczarni as lovable scoundrels who target the rich (and occasionally romance away their sons or daughters). Many victims of the Sczarni's schemes, of course, scoff at such glamorization of the organization's unscrupulous activities. Interestingly, some Sczarni members are followers

23

of Desna, due to her close association with Varisia, and often call on her for luck.

The wide variety of Sczarni groups and their usual aversion to violence means that many antiheroic characters would fit in well. They might be members of one of the Sczarni families, owe a debt to one, or hope to join, generally using their talents to prey on the rich and powerful rather than those struggling to get by. The Sczarni's typical type of business attracts quite a few rogues, but that is by no means the only class with abilities the Sczarni would appreciate; a wide variety of skills are welcomed among their ranks. Though those of Varisian heritage make up the majority of the organization, all that is required for membership is a flexible sense of morality. Joining the Sczarni can be immensely profitable, but it can also prove dangerous when dealing with rival groups or organizations opposed to the Sczarni, such as local law enforcement. Antiheroic characters involved with the Sczarni may run cons targeting the wealthy, carry out heists on noble estates, or blackmail the powerful to protect those who cannot fight back.

SLEEPLESS AGENCY

The mysterious Sleepless Agency is an organization composed of detectives and guards for hire that is headquartered in the city of Thrushmoor in southern Ustalav. It is headed by the enigmatic Cesadia Wrentz, and its agents are skilled at exposing corruption and finding lost people or items, though some may be less scrupulous than others. There are many rumors about the organization's actual goals, but little in the way of concrete information exists about the true intentions of the clandestine company. If the Sleepless Agency secretly has a nefarious agenda, it has been very thorough in covering its tracks, and most such rumors are dismissed as simply that. It does, however, have a reputation for being ruthless in completing its jobs, and some of the sleepless detectives have been known to engage in harassment, outright sabotage, and other ethically dubious methods of gathering information, even when the targets of interrogation pose no obvious threat. As such, antiheroic characters who believe that the ends justify the means would do quite well in the

agency, particularly those who seek to investigate crimes or mysterious happenings.

Antiheroic characters working for—or aiming to join—the Sleepless Agency are likely to have an investigative bent or be interested in working as muscle. Many sleepless detectives have levels in the prestige class of the same name (see page 52 of *Pathfinder Campaign Setting: Paths of Prestige*). Though the agency is highly organized, its sleepless detectives are given a great deal of freedom in their assignments; their methods are of no concern to the management, as long as the job gets done. Characters might wish to work with the agency to recover something or someone they've lost or because they have an enemy in common. A character seeking vengeance against a corrupt noble might come across a sleepless detective investigating that same noble or find himself on the trail of a cult that the agency is also seeking. Such a case could provide a natural entry point for a character to apply for membership.

Due to the number of jobs and intrigues the agency is involved in at any one time, it is entirely possible that its aims coincide with those of a character even if the character is not directly affiliated. In such cases, the character may end up at odds with the detective on that particular case if an arrangement to work together is not reached. This may result in a fight, an eventual alliance, or even an offer to work for the Sleepless Agency, if the character sufficiently impresses the detectives with her skills. Investigation is a dangerous business, and those who are both willing and able to engage in such work are not common; the Sleepless Agency is always on the lookout for new talent to hire.

WASP QUEENS

The Wasp Queens are an infamous organization—often dismissed as a wild tale—of elite female thieves who follow Calistria, focusing on her aspects of revenge and trickery. Though the Wasp Queens engage in a variety of activities for hire, the jobs they prefer are those said by others to be impossible. No member of the Wasp Queens can resist the lure of an ancient relic in a castle no one has ever broken into, a famous artifact of an ancient hero, or the well-guarded vaults of an Abadaran bank. Their stories are legendary throughout the Inner Sea region, with most of them spread by the Wasp Queens themselves, who are known for their braggadocio.

The group is currently led by Arala Insifaal, a mercurial half-elf who nurses an incredible grudge. All hopeful members must apply to her for consideration, though passing the tests she requires of candidates is by no means easy, and failure usually means death. There is very little margin for error in the Wasp Queens' business, after all, and those who can't measure up are better off not getting the chance.

The Wasp Queens accept only female members who are elven or half-elven, limiting true membership in the organization to characters of that background. Therefore, antiheroic characters who are female elves or half-elves and follow Calistria would be the best fit. Still, the group sometimes needs to call in outside expertise, though such freelance work is only for a specific job or goal and does not constitute membership. The Wasp Queens are often fraught with infighting and rivalries, and calling on allies not directly affiliated with the group is a good way for a member to get ahead of a rival while maintaining plausible deniability. They also occasionally call in outsiders to assist in dealing with an outside threat—one of the few things that can unify the group—particularly if there is suspicion that one of their own may be compromised. Because of the Wasp Queens' usual business, most who join the organization are thieves of some sort, though many are skilled at espionage, and a few are clerics or warpriests of Calistria. Antiheroic characters who join as full members or hire on for a freelance job have the opportunity to become infamous for their daring thefts—assuming they succeed.

ARCHETYPE

The following is an archetype for rogues who don't mind turning a blind eye to the operations of organizations—as long as there's profit involved.

DISCRETION SPECIALIST (ROGUE ARCHETYPE)

Often brought in to handle messy situations, discretion specialists deal with bodies, inconvenient witnesses, and other loose ends. Many organizations employ them to cover up activities that might be unpopular—should they become known to the general populace.

This archetype is appropriate for rogues built using either the *Pathfinder RPG Core Rulebook* or *Pathfinder RPG Pathfinder Unchained*.

Fast Talker (Ex): A discretion specialist adds half her rogue level (minimum +1) as a bonus on Bluff, Diplomacy, and Intimidate checks.

This replaces trapfinding.

Obfuscation (Su): A discretion specialist is highly skilled at convincing others not to trust their own senses. At 3rd level as a full-round action, the discretion specialist can convince one living creature within 30 feet that up to 5 minutes of its memories from the past hour are unreliable. If the target fails a Will saving throw (DC = 10 + half the discretion specialist's rogue level + her Intelligence

modifier), the target is convinced that those memories didn't happen or that it's confusing the memories with a dream (or is otherwise hazy as to the memories' reality). Each hour after the discretion specialist uses this ability, the target can attempt a new Will saving throw to realize that its relevant memories have been tampered with, although not necessarily that the discretion specialist was the originator of the tampering.

The discretion specialist can use this ability once per day, and one additional time per day for every 5 rogue levels she has. At 6th level and every 3 levels thereafter, the discretion specialist can obfuscate memories from an additional hour in the past (to a maximum of 6 hours at 18th level).

This replaces trap sense (for a core rogue) or danger sense (for an unchained rogue).

Evidence Disposal (Sp): A discretion specialist can cover up a corpse's cause of a death—or dispose of it entirely. At 4th level, the discretion specialist gains the ability to cast *dress corpse* (*Pathfinder RPG Ultimate Intrigue* 212) as a spell-like ability, using her rogue level as her caster level. She can use this ability once per day, plus one additional time per day for every 5 rogue levels she has (to a maximum of five times at 20th level).

At 12th level, she can spend two uses of this ability to disintegrate a corpse entirely as a full-round action, leaving behind only a trace of fine dust (a disintegrated creature's equipment is unaffected). The target cannot be an undead creature. A corpse disintegrated this way cannot be brought back to life except by *resurrection* or more powerful magic, including *miracle* or *wish*.

This replaces the rogue talents gained at 4th and 12th levels.

No Loose Ends (Ex): At 4th level, the discretion specialist can prevent opponents from escaping. Opponents damaged by the discretion specialist's sneak attack are unable to take the withdraw action for 1 round, though they can still move as normal.

At 8th level, a creature damaged by the discretion specialist's sneak attack is hampered in casting spells of the teleportation subschool (such as *dimension door*) as well as using methods of magical transport such as *shadow walk*. A target attempting to cast such a spell before the end of the discretion specialist's next turn must succeed at a concentration check (in addition to any concentration checks required for casting while threatened or other circumstances) or lose the spell. The DC of this check is equal to 10 + half the discretion specialist's rogue level + her Intelligence modifier.

This replaces uncanny dodge and improved uncanny dodge.

Rogue Talents: The following rogue talents complement this archetype: camouflage[APG], charmer[APG], convincing lie[UC], honeyed words[APG], and quick disguise[APG].

Advanced Talents: The following advanced talents complement this archetype: hide in plain sight[UC] and master of disguise[APG].

Heroic Organizations

While antiheroes fit well in groups that share their jaded outlook, they can also be found in more traditionally heroic organizations. Often, antiheroic members of such groups either are willing to go to extremes in fighting for their ideals or are allies of convenience whose goals coincide with the group's. The skills of an antihero can be very useful to a heroic organization, especially on missions that may not be officially sanctioned or openly acknowledged. In some cases, a heroic organization might hope to guide antiheroes along a morally upright path or keep their destructive tendencies in check through positive influences.

While gold and social connections are sound reasons for an antihero to work with a heroic organization, such alliances often involve more than purely practical gain. Antiheroes in heroic organizations engage in a balancing act between doing what they believe necessary and staying on their organization's good side. Many antiheroes truly believe in their causes and view the ends as justifying the means, even if great sacrifices must be made along the way. Others may hope to redeem themselves from a dark past and see working for a good cause as a way to do so.

BELLFLOWER NETWORK

The Bellflower Network is a secret society dedicated to freeing halfling slaves in Imperial Cheliax. Members of the Bellflower Network operate in isolated cells in order to prevent the entire organization's destruction if a cell is compromised. The leader of the Bellflower Network is known as the Farmer, a title passed down as leadership changes. Since the Bellflower Network often operates outside the law, antiheroes are especially welcome and may take a more merciless view of fighting slavery than other members. Many front-line members are halflings, but other races are also present in support roles, particularly when infiltrating slaving operations. An antihero in the Bellflower Network might assassinate slavers or those who own slaves, engage in sabotage against slaving rings, or smuggle slaves to safety.

EAGLE KNIGHTS OF ANDORAN

The Eagle Knights of Andoran are sworn to protect Andoran's interests and fight against slavery. As such, they often carry out clandestine operations. Of the Eagle Knights' branches, the Twilight Talons are the most likely to recruit antiheroes, though the others sometimes use them as well. As the Twilight Talons are not publicly acknowledged by the Andoren government, they have freer rein to carry out their assassination, espionage, and sabotage operations without causing diplomatic problems. They may require antiheroes to carry out the assassination of a prominent slaver or to go deep undercover in Egorian to spy on the court of Queen Abrogail, for example. If an antiheroic character joins the naval branch of the Eagle Knights—the Gray Corsairs—she may be tasked with raiding slave ships or engaging in piracy against ships of enemy nations. An antihero working for the Eagle Knights is likely Andoren or perhaps strongly believes in Andoran's ideals of freedom and equality. Depending on the branch in which she operates, her ruthless tendencies may be openly encouraged, or permitted only under the right circumstances.

KNIGHTS OF OZEM

The Knights of Ozem are a military order dedicated to Iomedae. Based in Lastwall, they are famous for having aided in the defeat of Tar-Baphon during the Shining Crusade. They now guard his prison of Gallowspire, destroy undead, and fight against demons in the Worldwound. As they are devoted to a lawful good goddess, they may not seem like a natural choice for an antihero, but even the high-minded knights need the benefit of morally questionable tactics on occasion. And though Iomedae herself does not necessarily focus on redemption, a good knight knows that sometimes a disreputable ally simply needs guidance to find the right path. An antihero might work to uncover corruption among crusaders in the Worldwound or root out cults devoted to the Whispering Way.

MAGAAMBYA

One of the largest arcane schools in the Inner Sea region, the Magaambya is a repository of historical records and practical knowledge from the Mwangi Expanse and beyond. The Magaambya's founding dates to thousands of years ago, when it was established by the legendary Old-Mage Jatembe. The school teaches a distinctive style of arcane magic that incorporates elements of druidism and nature worship, though controlling weather, interfacing with outsiders, scrying, and transforming into beasts all feature in the curricula. Locals and magic enthusiasts from all over Golarion travel to the Mwangi Expanse to attend the school. Beyond their primary role as educators, the Magaambya's masters also serve as protectors of the ancient knowledge that lies hidden in the ruins of the region's past civilizations. The masters often hire adventurers to explore these locales and bring back important relics and tomes, and an antihero might find a fine place as an excavator of such treasures, provided that she respects the antiquity of what she seeks and the authority of those who hire her. Further, the Magaambya's masters provide significant arcane defense for the surrounding region, and this protection often requires a good deal of espionage. Antiheroes who are former students or trusted allies might find solid work rooting out plots against the masters, stopping planned heists of priceless relics, or halting outside threats to the region before they can do any harm. The Magaambya doesn't tolerate outright evil in its hires, but there is almost always a place for an antihero whose methods are a little rough around the edges but who nonetheless gets important jobs done.

RUTHLESS AGENT (INVESTIGATOR ARCHETYPE)

Ruthless agents are often called upon for their skills at extracting information by any means necessary. Though some view their methods as extreme, ruthless agents prize getting the job done at all costs. Ruthless agents can be found in the employ of nearly any organization—even goodly groups whose leaders either don't know the extent of ruthless agents' zeal or are willing to look the other way to take advantage of these investigators' incredible efficiency.

Alignment: Any nongood.

This alters the investigator's alignment.

Inspiration (Ex): A ruthless agent focuses on reading motivations and using interrogation tactics. She can use inspiration on Intimidate, Knowledge, and Sense Motive checks without expending a use of inspiration, provided she's trained in the skill. A ruthless agent can't spend inspiration on attack rolls or saving throws.

This alters inspiration.

Enhanced Intimidation (Ex): A ruthless agent adds half her investigator level (minimum +1) as a bonus on Intimidate checks. When the ruthless agent uses Intimidate to influence an opponent's attitude, the duration of the attitude shift is 1d6×10 minutes per investigator level (rather than the normal 1d6×10 minutes).

Additionally, the ruthless agent is an expert in blending coercion and fear. The first time the ruthless agent attempts to use Intimidate to influence an opponent's attitude and fails, she can retry it against that same opponent with no increase to the DC. Subsequent attempts to influence the same opponent are subject to increased DCs as normal.

This replaces trapfinding.

Interrogate (Su): At 3rd level as a full-round action, a ruthless agent can ask a target one question for every 2 investigator levels she has. The target is not compelled to answer truthfully, but the ruthless agent's implicit or explicit threats and looming manner leads the target to believe the ruthless agent will cause it serious harm if it lies. This imposes a –2 penalty on the target's Bluff checks to lie when answering the specific questions the ruthless agent asked. At 6th level and every 3 levels thereafter, the penalty increases by 2 (to a maximum of –12 at 18th level). She can use this ability a number of times per day equal to 3 + her Intelligence modifier. This is a mind-affecting fear effect.

This replaces trap sense.

Agonizing Strike (Ex): At 4th level, a ruthless agent has learned how to finesse her attacks to discomfort a foe. When she deals damage using her studied strike, she can make this damage nonlethal (regardless of whether her weapon normally deals lethal or nonlethal damage), forcing the target to succeed at a Fortitude saving throw (DC = 10 + half the ruthless agent's level + her Intelligence modifier) or be sickened for 1 round and take a –2 penalty on Will saving throws for 1 minute. Multiple agonizing strikes do not worsen the condition or impose an additional penalty on Will saves, but they do increase the duration of both effects.

This replaces swift alchemy.

Concoction of Truth (Su): At 7th level, a ruthless agent automatically adds *discern lies* to her list of formulae known. She prepares this as a 3rd-level extract, and she can prepare one *discern lies* extract each day that does not count against her daily allotment of extracts.

This replaces the investigator talent gained at 7th level.

Compel Obedience (Sp): At 11th level, a ruthless agent can issue a binding command to a creature as a full-round action once per day. This command acts like *geas/quest* with the creature as the target, using the ruthless agent's investigator level as the caster level. The ruthless agent can compel obedience from only one creature at a time (as soon as the *geas/quest* is fulfilled, however, the ruthless agent can use this ability again, as long as she has a use of this ability available).

At 17th level, the ruthless agent can compel obedience from two creatures at once, and she is always aware of the targets as if they were under the effects of a *status* spell (caster level = the ruthless agent's investigator level).

This replaces the investigator talents gained at 11th and 17th levels.

Nasty Alchemy

Alchemy has long had a reputation for unpredictability and instability, so it's no surprise that many scoundrelly antiheroes make free use of alchemical tricks and tools. While there are certainly circumstances in which one could feasibly use the presented items in a noble fashion, those with a more mischievous bent more often employ them to sow chaos, cut corners, or create confusion or panic so they can slip away in the ensuing mayhem.

ALCHEMICAL REMEDY AND TOOL

Some alchemical items lend themselves especially for use by those with nefarious intent—or at least by those who thumb their noses at polite society. While even the most upright heroes might reluctantly employ underhanded tactics in dire situations, antiheroes do so without even thinking twice.

INIQUITOUS PANACEA	PRICE 200 GP
	WEIGHT 1 lb.

Although it's often packaged and sold as a cure-all, this nefarious snake-oil concoction temporarily weakens the immune system of whoever consumes it, accelerating the rate at which the drinker suffers from a contracted poison or disease.

Consuming the iniquitous panacea while suffering the effects of a disease or poison increases the DCs of the imbiber's next three Fortitude saving throws against the disease or poison by 2 and halves the remaining onset time of any contracted diseases or poisons that have not yet taken effect; these effects wear off after 24 hours. An iniquitous panacea has no effect on creatures that have not contracted a disease or a poison. Crafting an iniquitous panacea requires a successful DC 15 Craft (alchemy) check.

INK OF STOLEN SECRETS	PRICE 50 GP
	WEIGHT 1 lb.

This alchemically concocted black ink can be attuned to a standard sheet of parchment. Anything inscribed using the ink (anywhere on the same plane of existence) appears on the attuned parchment in a sparkling blue script that lasts 1 hour. There is enough ink in one vial to fill one sheet of parchment. The ink cannot duplicate any written magical effects, such as a symbol of death (as per the spell of the same name). Crafting a vial of ink of stolen secrets requires a successful DC 15 Craft (alchemy) check.

ALCHEMICAL WEAPONS

While those who strongly believe in fighting with dignity and honor might raise an eyebrow at the use of the following alchemical weapons, many antiheroes have no such qualms, reasoning that their ends justify any means they deem necessary—or entertaining.

DUNG GRENADE	PRICE 100 GP
	WEIGHT 1 lb.

The casing of this modified fuse grenade[UE] is partially filled with animal dung or guano. You can throw a dung grenade as a splash weapon with a range increment of 10 feet. Any creature directly hit by a dung grenade or in its splash radius takes 1d6 points of fire damage and is covered with the grenade's malodorous contents, becoming sickened for 1d4 rounds. A target can attempt a DC 15 Reflex saving throw to halve the damage and the duration of the sickened condition. Crafting a dung grenade requires a successful DC 25 Craft (alchemy) check.

HELLFIRE SPARKLER	PRICE 250 GP
	WEIGHT 50 lbs.

This large barrel-shaped sparkler is imbued with mysterious, hellish forces. The fuse can be lit as a standard action; 1d4 rounds later, the sparkler crackles violently with sickly-green sparks that take the form of an army of ferocious devils. Creatures within a 10-foot-radius burst take 3d6 points of fire damage and become shaken for 2 rounds; a target can attempt a DC 15 Will save to halve the damage and the duration of the shaken condition. Crafting a hellfire sparkler requires a successful DC 25 Craft (alchemy) check.

PORTABLE HIVE	PRICE 300 GP
	WEIGHT —

This large flask holds a swarm of angry wasps. A portable hive can be thrown as a splash weapon, and when it hits a grid intersection or a creature, a wasp swarm (Pathfinder RPG Bestiary 275) appears in a 10-foot-by-10-foot square at the point of impact. This swarm does not have the distraction or poison special abilities, and it disperses after 1d4 rounds. Crafting a portable hive requires a successful DC 25 Craft (alchemy) check.

POISONS

Even heroes who play fast and loose with the rules often steer clear of using poisons. Employing the toxins introduced below takes a special disregard for fair play—and securing them in the first place often requires shady contacts and unpleasant promises.

CONCENTRATED LAXATIVE	PRICE 75 GP
	WEIGHT —

Type poison, ingested; **Save** Fortitude DC 12
Onset 10 minutes; **Frequency** 1/minute for 2 minutes
Effect This mixture gained popularity—and notoriety—when Calistrians used it for elaborate pranks, but now tricksters of all stripes use the colonic concoction for any number of reasons, such as to incommode a nosy interlocutor. After the

first failed saving throw, the target is sickened for 1 minute, and after a second failure, the target is nauseated for 1 minute; **Cure** 1 save

FRIGHTSHADE	**PRICE** 100 GP
	WEIGHT —

Type poison, inhaled; **Save** Fortitude DC 14
Onset immediate; **Frequency** 1/round for 4 rounds
Effect This plant's pollen contains a powerful hallucinogen that causes affected creatures to experience terribly realistic visions of death and destruction. The target is shaken until the beginning of her next turn. When the target succeeds at her saving throw against the poison, or when the initial duration ends, she is shaken for an additional 1d4 rounds. (This is not a fear effect.); **Cure** 1 save

LEOPARD'S BANE	**PRICE** 4,500 GP
	WEIGHT —

Type poison, ingested; **Save** Fortitude DC 20
Onset 1 minute; **Frequency** 1/round for 6 rounds
Effect Consuming the flowers of this plant weakens the walls of the imbiber's veins, causing them to rupture. The target takes 1d2 points of Constitution drain and 1d4 points of bleed damage. Blood (or an equivalent bodily fluid, if the imbiber does not have blood) flows from the target's eyes, causing the subject to be blinded for the duration of the bleed effect. This bleeding can be stopped as normal (with a successful DC 15 Heal check or the application of any magical healing); **Cure** 2 saves

LIQUID LEPROSY	**PRICE** 750 GP
	WEIGHT —

Type poison, contact; **Save** Fortitude DC 20
Onset 1 minute; **Frequency** 1/minute for 6 minutes
Effect Each time the target fails its saving throw, part of his body begins to necrotize. Roll d% on the table below to determine which part of the body starts rotting. Each necrotizing effect stacks with the others but not with itself; if the same effect is rolled more than once, choose a new effect that hasn't been rolled yet from on the table; **Cure** 2 saves

d%	Effect
1–30	Hands, 2 Dex damage
31–60	Arms, 2 Str damage
61–95	Torso, 2 Con damage
96–100	Brain, 2 Int and 2 Wis damage

LUNGSAP POWDER	**PRICE** 1,200 GP
	WEIGHT —

Type poison, inhaled; **Save** Fortitude DC 16
Onset immediate; **Frequency** 1/round for 4 rounds
Effect This fine powder absorbs the oxygen from the lungs of any creature that breathes it in, causing the creature to gradually asphyxiate. The target has difficulty breathing and is staggered. If the target suffers the effect for 4 rounds, he falls unconscious for 1 minute at the end of the fourth round; **Cure** 1 save

SLOTH'S BITE	**PRICE** 300 GP
	WEIGHT —

Type poison, injury; **Save** Fortitude DC 18
Onset immediate; **Frequency** 1/round for 6 rounds
Effect This poison causes the affected creature to be sluggish and slow to react. The target takes 1d2 points of Dexterity damage and is flat-footed until the beginning of her next turn; **Cure** 1 save

ALCHEMIST DISCOVERIES

Alchemists are constantly looking for ways to push boundaries, often without concern for the reactions of others—or the potential for self-harm—and an antiheroic alchemist is no exception. Any alchemist who meets the prerequisites can take the following discoveries. Discoveries that modify bombs and that are marked with an asterisk (*) do not stack.

Bone-Spike Mutagen (Su): When the alchemist imbibes a mutagen, he mutates his skeletal structure, causing the bones on his elbows, knuckles, spine, and shoulder blades to grow massive and pierce his skin, exposing themselves as large spikes. While the mutagen is in effect, the alchemist's natural armor bonus granted by the mutagen increases by 2. The spikes count as masterwork armor spikes with which the alchemist is proficient. An alchemist must be at least 6th level before selecting this discovery.

Jury-Rigged Bomb* (Su): 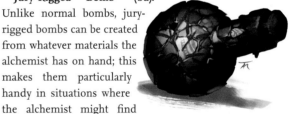 Unlike normal bombs, jury-rigged bombs can be created from whatever materials the alchemist has on hand; this makes them particularly handy in situations where the alchemist might find himself imprisoned or stripped of his equipment. Jury-rigged bombs can be crafted and thrown as a swift action (this counts against the alchemist's daily use of bombs), and they deal only 1d4 points of damage + additional damage equal to half the alchemist's Intelligence modifier on a direct hit. This damage increases by 1d4 at 3rd level and every 2 levels thereafter. Despite being useful in a pinch, jury-rigged bombs are nonetheless crudely crafted and highly unstable; if the alchemist's attack roll results in a natural 1, the bomb explodes as he is creating it, and he takes damage as if he had taken a direct hit. An alchemist must be at least 4th level before selecting this discovery.

Sand Bomb* (Su): When the 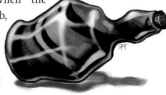 alchemist creates a bomb, he can pack the casing full of sand that explodes in an abrasive cloud on impact. A creature that takes a direct hit from a sand bomb is blinded for 1 round, as are any creatures in the splash radius that fail a Reflex save (DC = 10 + half the alchemist's level + his Intelligence modifier).

Antiheroic Magical Equipment

Whether working for a shady organization, seeking revenge, or just looking to make a little bit of coin, antiheroes use magic items for their efficacy and power. Antiheroic adventurers can make great use of the items presented here to achieve their goals; they just might need to leave town quickly if they do.

MAGIC ITEMS

Antiheroic adventurers appreciate the utility provided by most magic weapons and tools, but there are some items that prove especially irresistible to the irascible sort. Whether they present a way to subvert the expectations of the weak willed, get the upper hand in an underhanded way, or simply make the wielder look more impressive than he might actually be, these items are popular choices for the antiheroic bent.

ARROW SLICER		PRICE 21,310 GP
SLOT none	CL 6th	WEIGHT 2 lbs.
AURA moderate evocation		

The blade of this +1 limning short sword pulsates with a faint blue glow when wielded. When its wielder is targeted by ranged attacks, an arrow slicer shines even brighter, alerting its user of the incoming danger and granting a +2 bonus on Perception checks to act in the surprise round.

Once per round when the wielder is targeted by an attack from a ranged weapon that uses nonfirearm ammunition, he can attempt a DC 20 Reflex saving throw as an immediate action to deflect the projectile. If he exceeds the DC by more than 5, he not only deflects the projectile but also slices it in half, and all foes within 30 feet that can see the wielder do so become shaken for 1d4 rounds; this is a fear effect and can affect a given creature only once per day. Large projectiles, such as boulders hurled by giants and ballista bolts, can't be deflected or cut in half.

CONSTRUCTION REQUIREMENTS	COST 10,810 GP
Craft Magic Arms and Armor, faerie fire, wind wall^{UM}	

CROOK'S CUBE		PRICE 26,000 GP
SLOT none	CL 11th	WEIGHT 4 lbs.
AURA moderate divination		

This crystalline cube has a thin plate of soft white stone on one of its faces that's inscribed with several lines of cryptic runes. When the cube's bearer speaks a command word, the runes change shape and spell out information regarding nearby secrets such as back alleys and hidden paths.

Once per day, the wielder of a crook's cube can cast find the path. The cube also grants its wielder a +5 insight bonus on

checks with the following skills in which the wielder has at least 5 ranks: Knowledge (dungeoneering), Knowledge (engineering), Knowledge (geography), Knowledge (history), and Knowledge (local).

CONSTRUCTION REQUIREMENTS	COST 13,000 GP
Craft Wondrous Item; find the path; at least 5 ranks in Knowledge (dungeoneering), Knowledge (engineering), Knowledge (geography), Knowledge (history), or Knowledge (local)	

DESNA'S COIN		PRICE 8,000 GP
SLOT none	CL 5th	WEIGHT —
AURA faint abjuration		

This standard gold coin typically has two blank faces, but its owner can cause the holy symbol of Desna—a butterfly with the sun, the moon, and stars on its wings—to appear on either face at will. This proves especially useful when performing coin flips, as the owner of a Desna's coin can essentially guarantee that the result will end up in her favor.

As one would expect of an item associated with the goddess of luck, a Desna's coin confers on its owner an uncanny ability to fortuitously avoid sudden threats. As a result, its bearer gains a +2 luck bonus on Reflex saving throws.

CONSTRUCTION REQUIREMENTS	COST 4,000 GP
Craft Wondrous Item, divine favor	

GUNS OF THE TWIN DRAKES		PRICE 18,600 GP
SLOT none	CL 15th	WEIGHT 8 lbs.
AURA strong transmutation		

These paired firearms—a +1 flaming dragon pistol^{UE} and a +1 frost dragon pistol^{UE}—are ornately inscribed and carefully carved to resemble fire and ice drakes as a tribute to an infamous pair of quarreling drake siblings (though the names of the drakes have been lost to time).

As a swift action, the guns of the twin drakes can be joined together to function as a double-barreled weapon. As a standard action, the joined weapons can be fired at the same time; in this case they must be fired at the same target, and each shot uses a separate attack roll and takes a -4 penalty. When fired this way, the first shot deals 1d4 additional points of fire damage and the second deals 1d4 additional points of cold damage; this damage is instead of the extra damage normally granted by the flaming and frost weapon special abilities.

CONSTRUCTION REQUIREMENTS	COST 10,600 GP
Craft Magic Arms and Armor, haste, fireball, ray of frost	

LENSES OF THE BULLY		PRICE 12,500 GP
SLOT eyes	**CL** 3rd	**WEIGHT** —
AURA faint abjuration		

Commonly used by thugs, these dark-tinted lenses make the wearer appear threatening. The wearer gains a +2 competence bonus on Intimidate checks. Intelligent creatures find the wearer hard to read; the wearer is treated as if affected by a constant *undetectable alignment* spell, making her true motives difficult to ascertain.

CONSTRUCTION REQUIREMENTS	COST 6,250 GP
Craft Wondrous Item, *undetectable alignment*	

VIAL OF RECKLESS COURAGE		PRICE 5,000 GP
SLOT none	**CL** 5th	**WEIGHT** 1 lb.
AURA faint transmutation		

This small glass vial contains an effervescent blue liquid. When imbibed, a *vial of reckless courage* instills a sense of bravery in the drinker, granting a +4 enhancement bonus on saving throws against fear effects. If the drinker is under a fear effect, she can attempt a new saving throw with a +2 bonus. The drinker becomes eager to rush into danger, and as a result, all of her modes of movement (including burrow, climb, fly, and swim speeds) increase by 30 feet, to a maximum of double her normal speed in any given form of movement, for 5 rounds.

CONSTRUCTION REQUIREMENTS	COST 2,500 GP
Craft Wondrous Item, *haste*, *remove fear*	

SPECIFIC CURSED ITEMS

Antiheroes have no qualms about using cursed items—or foisting them onto others—to help them achieve their goals.

BLOODBITE		
SLOT none	**CL** 10th	**WEIGHT** 8 lbs.
AURA moderate evocation		

The grip of this greatsword has a series of deep notches, and its jagged blade is a deep crimson. A *bloodbite* is awakened by bloodlust, and its appetite must be sated. When the wielder makes a successful attack with the *bloodbite*, it inflicts a wound that deals 1d4 points of bleed damage (in addition to its normal damage), but it also deals 1d4 points of bleed damage to the wielder as the hilt grows teeth that dig into the wielder's hands. Once used, the *bloodbite* must be used as its wielder's primary melee weapon, and it can be discarded only after the owner benefits from a *remove curse* spell or similar effect.

INTENDED MAGIC ITEM
+2 wounding greatsword

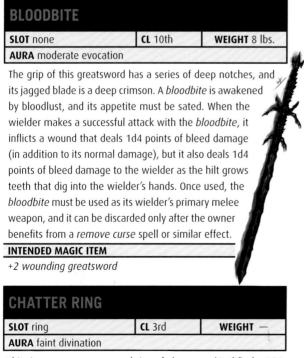

CHATTER RING		
SLOT ring	**CL** 3rd	**WEIGHT** —
AURA faint divination		

This ring appears as a normal *ring of eloquence* (*Pathfinder RPG Advanced Class Guide* 216), with four different languages (usually Common, Dwarven, Elven, and Gnome) etched around the inside of a silver band, and the wearer of a *chatter ring* gains the ability to speak the four languages inscribed in the ring. However, the difference between a *chatter ring* and a normal *ring of eloquence* quickly becomes apparent when the wearer speaks, as he becomes overwhelmingly talkative. The wearer takes a –2 penalty on Bluff, Diplomacy, Disguise, Perform (oratory), and Stealth checks. The ring can be removed only after the wearer benefits from a *remove curse* spell or similar effect.

INTENDED MAGIC ITEM
ring of eloquence^{ACG}

KLEPTOMANIAC'S GLOVES		
SLOT hands	**CL** 3rd	**WEIGHT** 1 lb.
AURA faint transmutation		

These simple calfskin gloves intensify the avaricious inclinations of their wearer. *Kleptomaniac's gloves* confer the same +5 competence bonus on Sleight of Hands checks as *gloves of larceny* (*Pathfinder RPG Ultimate Equipment* 237), but the first time the wearer attempts to take something from a given creature with a Sleight of Hand check, she must attempt another such check against that creature at the first available opportunity, whether or not the first attempt was successful. This increases the DC of the check by 10, as though the first attempt were a failure, and it imparts a –20 penalty on the check. *Kleptomaniac's gloves* can be removed only after the wearer benefits from a *remove curse* spell or similar effect.

INTENDED MAGIC ITEM
gloves of larceny^{UE}

OVERCHARGED STAFF		
SLOT none	**CL** 11th	**WEIGHT** 5 lbs
AURA moderate evocation		

This staff appears as a normal *staff of electricity*, except it is black instead of silver and electricity occasionally arcs along the shaft. The curse on this weapon alters the *shocking grasp*, *lightning bolt*, and *chain lightning* spells granted by the staff, causing extra surges of energy to damage the wielder and his allies.

When the wielder uses the *overcharged staff* to cast *shocking grasp*, he takes 1d3 points of electricity damage per caster level (maximum 5d3). When the wielder uses the *overcharged staff* to cast *lightning bolt*, a random ally takes 1d6 points of electricity damage per caster level (maximum 10d6); the ally takes half that amount with a successful Reflex save. When the wielder uses the *overcharged staff* to cast *chain lightning*, for each target the wielder chooses as a primary or secondary target, a random ally must be chosen as a secondary target.

INTENDED MAGIC ITEM
staff of electricity^{UE}

Next Month

The mysteries of witchcraft are compelling—even if they're taboo. From changelings who've inherited the blood of hags and witches whose patrons provide power at a price, to occult rituals that harness the power of hag covens and curses beyond the ken of most adventurers, *Pathfinder Player Companion: Blood of the Coven* offers a cauldron of options for characters steeped in the supernatural. Bewitching magic items and tips and tools for witch hunters ensure you'll have everything you need for a game steeped in the unknown!

WOULD YOU LIKE TO KNOW MORE?

They might not be the bravest or most selfless heroes, but antiheroes know how to achieve their ends at any cost, perhaps even using tactics others might find distasteful. Add a dash of the practical—and the dastardly—into your character's repertoire with these products that complement *Pathfinder Player Companion: Antihero's Handbook*!

An antihero fits seamlessly into intrigue-themed games—and *Ultimate Intrigue* provides robust rules for your character's daring heists, verbal duels, and other high-stakes games of shadows and secrets!

Immerse your antiheroes in the many cloak-and-dagger plots detailed in *Inner Sea Intrigue*, from the infamous thieves' guild of Absalom to the rebel networks of Galt to the secret courts of storied Taldor!

If fighting and dying honorably isn't your character's idea of fun, outfit her with the deliciously devious tips, tricks, and rules options in *Dirty Tactics Toolbox* to make sure that her opponents never have a fair chance!